WHAT SHALL I DO?
QUESTIONS AND ANSWERS IN CARDIOLOGY

What Shall I Do?
Questions And Answers
In
Cardiology

Roger Blackwood
MA, BM, BCh, MRCP

– and –

Bev Daily
MB, BS

To Keith Evans

Best Wishes

Bev Daily

BEACONSFIELD PUBLISHERS LTD
Beaconsfield, Bucks, England

First published in 1988

British Library Cataloguing in Publication Data
Blackwood, Roger
  What shall I do? : questions and answers in cardiology.
  1. Cardiology – Problems, exercises, etc.
  I. Title   II. Daily, Bev
  616.1'2'0076   RC682
  ISBN 0–906584–20–5

DRUGS

Proprietary names of the drugs discussed in this book are written with an initial capital letter, while generic names are written in small letters. The doses suggested are offered as guidelines, subject in every case to the individual user's clinical discretion and the manufacturer's current recommendations.

Medical illustrations by Barbara Hyams

Phototypeset by Gem Graphics, Trenance, Mawgan Porth, Cornwall, in 10 on 12 point Times.

Printed in Great Britain at the University Printing House, Oxford.

Introduction

As doctors we are continually required to answer questions. Some we answer in an assured manner with self-confidence. Others we answer in an assured manner, fingers firmly crossed behind our backs.

Technology moves along. We try to keep up. One no longer hears of Grandad's pacemaker blowing up at the crematorium, making Handel's 'Largo' sound more like the '1812 Overture'. Everybody has heard of that one. But what about 'Can my pacemaker be affected by microwaves?', 'What happens if it stops working?', 'How long do the batteries last?' Questions like that might cause a moment of hesitation and cerebral rummaging.

Unfortunately, most textbooks do not answer questions. They describe the disease, its pathology, signs, symptoms, outcome and treatment – but generally they do not give much in the way of advice.

This book consists entirely of questions and, hopefully, answers. There are three types of questions and they often cover the same topics from different points of view. Firstly, the kind of question regarding the pacemaker described above. The kind of question a patient asks his doctor. 'How soon can I drive after a heart attack?', 'Can my child with a hole in the heart have a typhoid injection?', 'Do I need to let the driving licence people know I've got heart trouble?'

Secondly, the kind of question that the GP might ask a cardiologist: 'Is there any place nowadays for using methyldopa?', 'What is the best analgesic for severe coronary pain in a patient with chronic obstructive airways disease?', 'When should I use intravenous atropine?'

And thirdly, the 'Your guess is as good as mine' type of question. The old chestnut about finding 10p and keeping it, and finding a bundle of fivers and taking it to the Police Station. But what about a one pound coin, or a five pound note, or two five pound notes? The 'Do I? Don't I?' type of question where only experience, feel and instinct can be of any use. These are the types of questions you might ask the cardiologist over a drink at medical society meetings. Not expecting the perfect answer, not even an answer that other cardiologists would necessarily agree with, but at least *an* answer given after consideration and thought, from a background of specialist experience.

This is therefore not a book to be studied under the illumination of midnight oil, but more designed to jog the neurones into thought, and perhaps even irritation . . . 'Rubbish!'

It does not in any way intend to cover but a small fraction of the vast field of cardiology. It does seek to ask many of the questions, however, to which the GP and the specialist might be exposed.

We would like to acknowledge our indebtedness to the following colleagues, each of whom made time to work through the first draft and whose informed and thoughtful comments we were able to take into account when preparing the final version: Dr Kim Fox, Dr Derek Maclean, Dr John Lloyd Parry and Dr Lewis Ritchie.

R.B., B.D.

Contents

'What shall I do?', said a tiny mole,
'A fairy has tumbled into my hole.
It is full of water and crawling things,
And she can't get out 'cos she's hurt her wings.'

Children's poem

Angina and Similar

1. **At 8 a.m. a man of fifty with no previous significant medical history has a typical cardiac pain lasting approximately twenty minutes. It is not severe. His GP is called to see him. An ECG is normal. His daughter is to be married at 12 midday. What advice would you give?**

This is an awful question to answer, because one's natural instinct is to let him go to his daughter's wedding. However, if he has a history typical of cardiac pain, you have no alternative but to assume it could be a myocardial infarction and send him into hospital. Some practitioners might keep such a patient at home, but that is a personal decision. Cardiac pain is notoriously difficult to diagnose and there is no way of being certain about pain of this type without serial ECG and serum enzyme measurements. (A normal first ECG can be a deadly trap for the unwary.) In this particular situation the patient may refuse admission, but your advice must be clear.

2. **Under what circumstances would you advise coronary angiography to a man of forty-five who has *occasional* stress- or exercise-induced chest pain? Under what circumstances would you not advise such an investigation?**

Coronary angiography is performed for specific reasons and not just as 'another test'. The most important reason for doing so is when cardiac surgery is contemplated. In a man under the age of forty-five, however, the investigation may be necessary for diagnostic reasons, particularly with regard to his occupation.

Coronary artery bypass grafting is performed for *pain*. In this particular patient's case, where pain is only an infrequent feature, it would seem unjustified. Occasionally, however, in the presence of left main stem disease (see Question 66) there may be a critical lesion without very much pain. This must be suspected if, during an exercise test, the ST segment drops very quickly, e.g. at a heart rate of around 100 per minute, and is associated with pain and, possibly, a fall in blood pressure.

1

Considering that the surgical five-year survival in a patient with left main stem disease is 90%, compared with the 60% survival in one medically treated, bypass surgery is almost mandatory. Although left main stem disease is uncommon, it is such a critical lesion that one must always consider it as a possibility. In the absence of a strongly positive exercise test, angiography would be performed if there was any doubt about the diagnosis.

Chest pain typical of angina can occur with aortic stenosis and cardiomyopathy, and if there is a question of whether or not the coronary arteries are at fault, angiography alone will give the answer.

In particular occupations – that of airline pilots for example – it is essential to define, precisely, the cause of any chest pain that might be experienced. In such cases, where loss of licence due to suspected heart disease is followed by loss of livelihood, it is entirely reasonable to request angiography. Some authorities suggest that any patient under the age of forty-five suffering from angina should have angiography, because left main stem disease might, occasionally, be missed. In the NHS, as it exists at present, this is simply not practicable. In summary, angiography is indicated for:

1) Pain.
2) Suspected left main stem disease.
3) If the patient's livelihood is at risk.

3. A young man of twenty-five consults his doctor about a precordial ache. 'Could it be my heart?' Is there an age below which you would *not* consider myocardial ischaemia in the differential diagnosis of chest pain?

No, but myocardial infarction is very uncommon in men under thirty and women under forty. Plaques of atheroma can be found in children's arteries from the age of three. By the teenage years, 50% of Western males have significant narrowings. Myocardial infarction, caused by congenitally abnormal coronary arteries, can occur in children but it is extremely rare.

In very young patients, e.g. teenagers, there have been reports of myocardial infarction in exceptional circumstances. Sniffing cocaine stimulates adrenaline to a degree which on occasions has precipitated an infarction; servicemen in extreme conditions of cold or heat, and travellers who have been severely dehydrated by gastroenteritis, have also been known to have a myocardial infarction. In very young people it is important to ascertain such a history if they present with chest pain. (Very occasionally a rare condition, homozygous hypercholesterolaemia, may be present and can be found by a simple blood test.)

There should be an increased suspicion of myocardial infarction in men aged between thirty and forty who smoke and who have a strong family history of heart disease. Although myocardial infarction is still uncommon in woman before the menopause, it should be suspected in those of a younger age group who have a family history of premature heart disease, who smoke and who take oral contraceptives.

4. Is lack of anginal symptoms in a man with known ischaemic heart disease whilst performing acts that might be considered detrimental, e.g. exercise such as skiing in very cold weather, evidence that he is doing himself no harm? Or is he putting himself at increased risk, in spite of the lack of pain?

Anginal pain is a warning sign of ischaemia. Its absence in ischaemia is less well understood. In the last few years much has been written about 'silent' ischaemia, i.e. evidence of ST segment changes on an ECG in the absence of pain. Analysis suggests that true ischaemia is occurring. What, then, are our practical guidelines?

1) In chronic stable angina where the pain can be readily reproduced at a certain workload (e.g. walking 400 yards), it is reasonable to assume this patient will always have a warning sign and that gentle skiing in reasonable weather is therefore OK.
2) If angina occurs at rest or at variable amounts of exercise, e.g. one day at 10 yards, another at 800 yards, there is too much uncertainty about the ischaemic heart disease to allow the patient to go skiing.
3) In general, any patient with ischaemic heart disease must avoid extremes of exercise, emotion or cold, whether they get angina or not.

5. A patient with angina is going to Switzerland on holiday. Normally the angina is well controlled. He wishes to go by train up the Jungfrau to 11,500 feet. Would you advise him against this?

Yes. The arterial oxygen saturation remains normal up to 6000 feet. High-altitude pulmonary oedema is known to occur from 8000 feet upwards in the unacclimatised patient, although it would be highly unlikely below 10,000 feet. As the oxygen saturation falls, ventilation increases along with the cardiac output. In general, therefore, any angina patient would be unwise to ascend (particularly acutely) beyond 8000 feet or so, and certainly not to 11,500 feet as the question asks (Figure 1). It is true that acclimatisation occurs, but this may be after the patient has had his myocardial infarction.

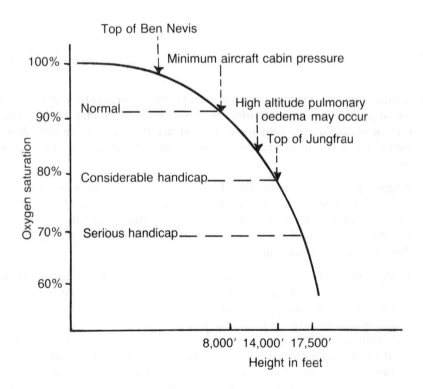

Figure 1 *Physiological reaction to altitude.*

4

6. **It is said that anybody given sufficient stimulation can be pushed across the epileptic threshold into having an epileptic fit. Is it possible for anybody to have an attack of angina given the right circumstances, e.g. altitude, extreme effort, oxygen lack?**

No. Angina will only occur if there is narrowing of the coronary arteries, spasm of the coronary arteries, Syndrome X (see Questions 8 and 95), aortic stenosis or hypertrophic obstructive cardiomyopathy; i.e. some existing pathology must be present. In the 1930s it was considered that you could damage your heart by excessive exercise, but this has been disproved unequivocally. Extremes of effort or altitude etc. will make a normal person lose consciousness but will not precipitate angina.

7. **Under what circumstances would you advise a man with angina to change his occupation? Under what circumstances would you advise a man with hypertension to change his occupation?**

Being told that he *must* change his occupation is surely one of the most devastating pieces of news that a man will ever receive. It must never be done casually, and only then if it is either legally essential or the need is very obvious to both doctor and patient. Indications may be divided into absolute (legal), relative and occasional. Taxi drivers are included in this category, although they hold a different licence. Commercial and armed services pilots are governed by different regulations and do not fall within the scope of this discussion.

Absolute indications to change a job apply to Heavy Goods Vehicle (HGV), Public Service Vehicle (PSV) and private pilot's licence holders only.

1) Angina. Any patient who has clinical angina or a positive exercise tolerance test may not have a licence. In addition, an abnormal resting ECG and an enlarged heart on X-ray (cardiothoracic ratio <0.50) precludes holding a licence. The other preclusion is evidence, at any time, of a previous myocardial infarction. If the patient's job depends on holding such a licence he must, by law, change to something else. After a series of stringent tests the patient may be able to regain his HGV or PSV licence after coronary artery bypass grafting. Very similar rules apply to holders of a private pilot's licence.

2) Hypertension. Holders of PSV, HGV, or private pilot's licences will lose them if their blood pressure remains above 200/110 despite treatment. For driving, beta-blockers and diuretics are acceptable, but not the more potent antihypertensives. In the case of flying the rules are tighter and the reader is referred to the Civil Aviation Authority.

Relative indications. Any job, particularly one involving driving, or working with dangerous machinery, or one which easily provokes angina, must be an indication for change. Both shift work and heavy manual work may not produce angina or worsen hypertension directly, but because of the fatigue and stress they induce they may make symptoms appear at the end of the shift or day. The majority of patients will initiate the change themselves but they will, most probably, also seek the doctor's advice. Those patients with hypertension who are prone to funny turns, lightheadedness or faintness also come into this category. In addition, if tranquillisers are required to control hypertension, fortunately a rare situation, changing jobs may be very beneficial.

Occasional indications. Occasionally patients become convinced that a change of job will improve their hypertension or angina. They may be correct, largely on psychological grounds, and each individual case has to be assessed on its own merits.

8. **In some patients angina appears to run a benign course. The patients can live for many years with no obvious worsening and without myocardial catastrophe. Is this a recognisable group and do the members of it have anything in common?**

We have all heard of the granny who lived to the age of eighty-five after developing angina at the age of forty-five and equally we know of many who have dropped dead without warning. Angina has a highly variable clinical spectrum with no specific groups (Figure 2). This is probably because angina may be caused by fixed narrowings of the coronary arteries, spasms of the coronary arteries, and a situation in which the myocardial cells themselves appear to be abnormal. In this condition, known as 'Syndrome X', the patient has angina with normal coronary arteries and no evidence of spasm. No doubt other causes of angina will be found; until all such causes are known, no definable groups will emerge from the prognostic point of view.

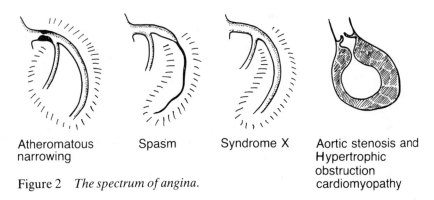

| Atheromatous narrowing | Spasm | Syndrome X | Aortic stenosis and Hypertrophic obstruction cardiomyopathy |

Figure 2   *The spectrum of angina.*

In the group with true atheroma, the following factors would suggest a poor prognosis: extensive atheroma, poor LV function, old age; as well as risk factors such as heavy smoking, hypercholesterolaemia and poorly-controlled hypertension.

9. If the two were to conflict, would you make a diagnosis of classical angina more on the history given or more on the results of an exercise tolerance test?

The diagnosis of classical angina is made on the history, not on tests. Angina is central chest pain coming on during exercise or emotion and disappearing afterwards in two to three minutes. It is worse in cold weather, after a big meal or in windy conditions. If at an exercise test there are no ECG changes, but typical pain as just described, the patient has angina. The opposite situation is difficult to interpret, i.e. the positive exercise test in an asymptomatic patient. At least 20% are reported to be falsely positive, and all one can do in this situation is weigh up each patient individually. If there are many risk factors, in particular a strong family history and smoking, then a small dose of a beta-blocker is justified. If there are no risk factors it is worth repeating the exercise test every six months. On many occasions, in my experience, a repeat exercise test is negative. In younger patients, referral for further investigation may be justified to make a definitive diagnosis.

If you have diagnosed classical angina clinically and the exercise test is negative, there is no need to keep re-exercising until you get the right result.

The exercise test is valuable prognostically. If it is very positive it suggests one should consider angiography. If it is negative one certainly would not. Once classical angina has been diagnosed most patients will end up on beta-blockers, plus sublingual GTN for an attack. Because beta-blockers produce an artificial slowing of the heart rate, another exercise test is of questionable value. Nevertheless, in an ideal world, we would probably repeat the exercise test in a patient with angina every two to three years, but this is impractical in the NHS. It should certainly be repeated if the anginal pains get worse, because then one would consider surgery, but *not* if the pains come on at rest (unstable angina). Exercising a patient with unstable angina is very dangerous.

10. **Is it or isn't it ? The bane of a GP's life. Is Mrs Brown's chest discomfort something to worry about? The symptoms are equivocal. They are relieved as much by her own indigestion medicine as by the doctor's GTN. Is there any simple test that might differentiate hiatus hernia pain from cardiac pain?**

No, I only wish there was. Two simple tests are often employed – giving GTN and either an antacid or an H_2 blocker. GTN helps angina but also relaxes smooth muscle. Pain resulting from a hiatus hernia may be due to oesophagitis but it can also be caused by oesophageal spasm. As GTN relaxes smooth muscle, so it may also relieve the pain caused by oesophageal spasm.

To complicate matters further, indigestion medicines can relieve angina. A belch, resulting from a good dose of such medication, in some curious way, often makes the angina sufferer feel much better.

If the diagnosis is unclear the patient needs both an exercise test and endoscopy. Even then there might be no clear answer, as angina patients often seem to have a hiatus hernia as well. Oesophageal spasm is notoriously difficult to diagnose, although drinking ice-cold water can often bring relief and hence is diagnostically helpful. Attempts have been made to reproduce the pain that the patient experiences using dilute hydrochloric acid by mouth, but the results are far from accurate. It just goes to show how little we really do know about the pathophysiology of angina.

Myocardial Infarction

11. In what position would you place a patient suffering from a myocardial infarction who has both dyspnoea *and* a low BP?

What matters to the patient at the lower end of the BP scale is not the blood pressure but the blood flow. You can clamp an aorta in two places and have a measurable pressure between the clamps but, of course, no flow. The position of the patient with low BP after a myocardial infarction is not therefore critical. He is unlikely to feel lightheaded, and as long as he is making adequate amounts of urine his blood flow will be considered sufficient, whatever his apparent blood pressure.

If the patient is dyspnoeic immediately after a myocardial infarction he has got pulmonary oedema and will feel much better in the sitting position. If he lies down he may 'drown' with pulmonary oedema because of the large increase in venous return. Whatever the blood pressure he should sit up and, if possible, receive oxygen. In many cases large amounts of catecholamines will be released, causing peripheral vasoconstriction. This could result in a falsely low blood pressure reading.

12. As a cardiologist, if you were to suffer a myocardial infarction would you prefer to be treated in hospital or at home? What circumstances might make you change your mind?

The 'Hospital versus Home' argument for myocardial infarction has raged for years. Senior nurses, anxious to reduce high technology, have often quoted three trials on this subject. In Bristol, Nottingham and Newcastle attempts were made to resolve the problem, and in each case there was no significant difference in the mortality between hospital and home treatment. However, there were serious omissions in these trials, the most important being that seriously ill patients were not included. This was a vital flaw.

Those with complications will only stand a chance if they are near to the 'high tech'. At present the majority of younger patients (under 65 years) are treated in hospital because it is there that they have the best chance. The idea that going into a coronary care unit causes more aggravation and worry than staying at home is largely nonsense. The modern young man having his coronary will have watched numerous television programmes on saving lives after myocardial infarction, and would be scared stiff to be left at home.

The choice between home and hospital is largely a social one. Many patients will expect to go to hospital, others will ask to stay at home. Some wives would be terrified to have their husband at home after a myocardial infarction, whereas in the older patient the need for the husband and wife to be together becomes overwhelming.

Sometimes the facilities at home are quite inappropriate. Wealthy patients might be able to employ a nurse for a week. After the age of 65 there seems little to be gained in mortality terms, complications or not, between home and hospital and this is certainly true forty-eight hours after the event.

What would I do? I would go to my own hospital unless the infarction had occurred more than two days earlier. I would enjoy the diamorphine, pretend I had more pain and ask for a second dose, and insist on my daily quota of Scotch. I would not set foot in my Outpatients for six weeks.

13. A distinguished cardiologist once said that thirty minutes after the onset of a myocardial infarction a patient is convalescent. Any comments?

This must have been quite a long time ago. Infarctions evolve over twenty-four hours or so. Once the clot has formed, part of the myocardium dies and it is surrounded by an area of injured myocardium. This area may die or survive. If the patient spends this time at work running up and down the stairs the 'salvageable' area will die. If the patient rests quietly this area may survive.

There have been many attempts to salvage myocardium in this situation since the mid 1970s. Beta-blockers, calcium antagonists, nitrates, hyaluronidase, 100% oxygen, aortic balloon pumping, vasodilators and urgent bypass grafting have all been tried, but because it is so difficult to prove that any good has actually been done, results have been disappointing. Beta-blockers probably are of value, but perhaps the most sensible thing is bed rest for the first forty-eight hours. After that the patient is most certainly convalescent.

The concept suggested in this question probably refers to the electrical deaths, 50% of which happen in the first hour after infarction. But primary ventricular fibrillation, a condition in which resuscitation is often successful, can occur at any time in the first twenty-four hours after infarction.

14. **A man who has had a heart attack some years before is referred to the cardiology Outpatients for vague, probably muscular, pains in the chest . . . 'to be on the safe side'. The report from the hospital says that further tests will be carried out but that the ECG shows evidence of an old infarction. How does the ECG of an old infarction differ from one showing present ischaemia?**

The ECG changes representing ischaemia or myocardial damage are as follows:

Q waves = Dead myocardium
Raised ST segments = Injured myocardium
Inverted T waves = Ischaemic myocardium
Tall pointed symmetrical T waves = Ischaemic myocardium

When a patient has a myocardial infarction there is a sequence of ECG changes.

Immediately: The ECG may be normal. Occasionally changes may occur as soon as the clot forms or even before (Figure 3).

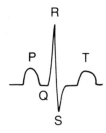

Figure 3   *The normal ECG.*

0-2 hours: The ST segments rise as the occluded artery forms the injury pattern (Figure 4).

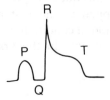

Figure 4   *Immediate injury pattern.*

3-8 hours: The injured area may be surrounded by an ischaemic area and itself surrounds a 'dead' area. Thus there may be Q waves, raised ST segments and inverted T waves at this time (Figure 5). A Q wave must be at least one small square wide (0·04 sec) to be pathological.

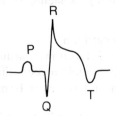

Figure 5   *A full thickness infarction pattern.*

8-24 hours: The injured tissue either dies or recovers leaving Q waves and inverted T waves (Figure 6).

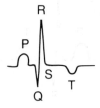

Figure 6   *Late infarction pattern.*

1-2 days: The T waves may, or may not, revert to normal but the Q waves remain for ever (Figure 7).

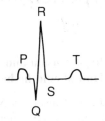

Figure 7   *Permanent infarction pattern.*

The answer to the question, therefore, is that an old infarction is usually represented by Q waves alone. Q waves in leads II, III and aVF represent an old inferior infarction, in leads I and aVL an old lateral infarction, and in the V leads, an old anterior infarction. The presence of raised ST segments represents an acute injury pattern, and inverted T waves an acute ischaemic episode.

15. **At the inquest of a male diabetic, fifty years old, killed in a car crash, the pathologist reports that there was evidence of a fairly recent myocardial infarction. As far as is known there was no history of chest pain. How common are silent infarctions? Are they truly silent or is it likely that the patient regarded the attack as an event of no great significance, e.g. indigestion?**

True silent infarctions are said to occur in up to 10% of the myocardial infarction population as a whole, and probably more often in the elderly. In diabetics, however, they constitute 20%. This lack of pain is presumably a consequence of neuronal damage. Many infarctions may be associated with mild symptoms but some give rise to no symptoms whatsoever.

What is important is that many patients who have a full-blown, painful, classical infarction will have had warning signs of discomfort or 'indigestion' for some months beforehand. Checking such patients, and encouraging middle-aged men, in particular, to go to the doctor if they have these warning signs, is vital if preventative medicine is to be successful.

Hypertension

6. A middle-aged man with hypertension and a passion for Purcell is intent on learning the trumpet. How should he be advised?

Playing the trumpet produces Valsalva's Manoeuvre. Clinically, this is expiring against a closed glottis. The increased intrathoracic pressure initially adds to the pressure of blood in the aorta, giving a small rise in blood pressure. The blood pressure then falls as the continued raised intrathoracic pressure compresses the veins and reduces the preload. Concomitant with this fall in blood pressure is a rise in heart rate and an increase in peripheral resistance. When the raised intrathoracic pressure ceases, as the Valsalva's Manoeuvre ends, the peripheral resistance remains high for ten seconds or so, resulting in a temporary rise in blood pressure. This sudden rise is accompanied by a relative bradycardia (Figure 8).

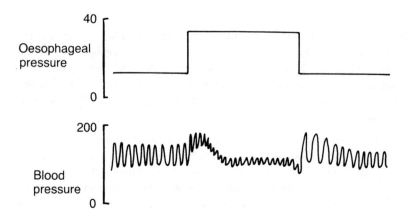

Figure 8   *The Valsalva manoeuvre.*

Thus a man with high blood pressure, not taking antihypertensives, can raise his blood pressure to a very high level indeed during a Valsalva manoeuvre. If he were to be playing a trumpet the Valsalva would be

14

repeated frequently and, at times, become almost continuous. He should therefore not be advised to play the trumpet voluntarily. However, if his blood pressure is controlled by medication there should be no more risk to him than to a person who is normotensive.

Fortunately there are not many aspiring Louis Armstrong hypertensives. But there are a great number of constipated ones. Not as tuneful, but using the same mechanisms and facing the same hazards.

17. At what level of hypertension, either diastolic or systolic, would you admit a 50-year old woman to hospital as an emergency?

It is probably unnecessary to admit a patient to hospital on blood pressure grounds alone. If the BP is 250/150 there is a tendency to feel that the patient's 'head will blow off'. The patient is admitted to hospital as an emergency for a lowering of blood pressure which will, it is hoped, prevent a cerebrovascular or cardiovascular catastrophe. In fact, the growing awareness of the dangers of cerebral oedema resulting from rapidly lowering the blood pressure have made this practice almost a thing of the past.

Gone are the days of crashing down the blood pressure in thirty minutes with intravenous hydralazine. Most patients will now be given a beta-blocker or other drugs *orally* with the intention of dropping the pressure towards normal in twenty-four hours. Because intravenous treatment is not required, hospital admission is no longer justified on that account alone.

Are there circumstances in which a CVA might be prevented? If on examination there is evidence of papilloedema or neurological deficit, there is a chance that it could be. The use of mannitol to produce an osmotic diuresis, or dexamethasone to reduce cerebral oedema, may be indicated if hypertensive encephalopathy is developing. Thus admission in this kind of circumstance is very important. In any case, hospital admission may be necessary if the neurological problem is severe. A cardiovascular accident might only be preventable by beta-blockade, which is part of the routine treatment anyway.

In conclusion. Admit if there is a high diastolic BP (say >120) plus papilloedema, or if there is evidence of hypertensive encephalopathy, chest pain, heart failure or palpitations. Ultimately it is always an individual decision for each patient.

18. **A patient is referred by a local optician as having hypertensive retinopathy. You confirm this on examination. The patient's age is 52. The BP is 140/90. The next week the BP is 145/90. There is neither sugar nor albumen in the urine. Do you take any action?**

This is a curious situation. If there really is at least Grade II hypertensive retinopathy one cannot help feeling that the sphygmomanometer you are using is in need of a service. If this is not the case, then the blood pressure must be labile, and at times very high, such as would occur in a phaeochromocytoma. This can be diagnosed by a urine test on a 24 hours sample, and most hospitals offer this service. If this test is negative, it is important to document the blood pressure over a period of time, preferably three or four times a day over two to three weeks. This can be done in hospital, but with beds being so tight alternatives are sought. At Wexham Park Hospital we give patients an automatic digital sphygmomanometer (cost circa £60) and ask them to record their findings. As long as the patient has an IQ greater than 60 this is not difficult. The recording should be checked in Outpatients with your own sphygmomanometer, both before the patient takes the machine away and when he returns. If the BP is labile, a beta-blocker is probably the best treatment.

19. **It is said that to allow a hypertensive with an epistaxis to continue to bleed only results in an anaemic hypertensive. Is it an advantage for a hypertensive not to have too high a haemoglobin and PCV? If so, should one think twice before prescribing a diuretic, thereby producing a degree of haemoconcentration?**

The level of PCV in hypertension can be very important. If it is too high there is definitely an increased risk of cerebrovascular accident. Notice must be taken if it exceeds 54% in men or 52% in women. In these circumstances, ideally, a red cell mass estimation should be performed. If this is raised, venesection is essential. This particular test, however, is not universally available and a decision based on symptoms must be made.

Evidence regarding transient ischaemic attacks (a stroke lasting less than twenty-four hours), ischaemic heart disease, particularly angina and peripheral vascular disease, suggest that polycythaemia is an important risk factor. It is therefore now believed that the nearer to 45% or below that the PCV can be maintained, the better. Most high PCVs are the result of stress polycythaemia, e.g. induced by smoking, hypertension or emotional stress. Control of these is the first-line management of the problem. If this fails to reduce the PCV, venesection must be considered. Because many of these patients are 'at risk' medically, venesection should only be performed in hospital.

A mild dose of diuretic, e.g. bendrofluazide 5mg or frusemide 20mg, is unlikely to alter the PCV, although higher doses most certainly can, and it would be inadvisable to prescribe them in a patient with polycythaemia unless absolutely necessary.

20. **Mr Smith has been taking blood pressure pills for seven years since he was found to be hypertensive at a routine medical examination. Several readings were taken over three weeks before essential hypertension was diagnosed and treatment started. He does not like taking pills and asks if he still needs them. How frequently does essential hypertension resolve itself? How long after the blood pressure has returned to normal is it worth reducing medication to see if it is still required? Are there any circumstances where you would leave well alone?**

Essential hypertension rarely, if ever, resolves itself. Once a patient has high blood pressure it is usually there for life. When the blood pressure is satisfactorily controlled it is better for the patient to stay on regular medication than to 'stop it and see'. This exercise is only occasionally successful and can be most dispiriting to the patient who has to start the treatment all over again.

If symptoms such as lightheadedness suggest drug-induced hypotension, treatment may need to be changed. In this situation a trial of withdrawing drug therapy may be worthwhile.

21. What parameters are used to decide whether a patient with hypertension is fit to have a heavy goods licence or a public service vehicle licence?

Certain cardiac conditions prohibit the holding of an HGV or PSV licence (see Question 7). If at any time the blood pressure is found to be 200/110 or above, the licence should be withdrawn until it is satisfactorily controlled, e.g. 150/90. Hypertension controlled by beta-blockers or diuretics is acceptable, but more potent antihypertensive agents which may cause dizziness or syncope are not generally allowed.

The reaction to antihypertensive agents is very important. A person experiencing dizziness, lightheadedness, drowsiness or blackouts would certainly not be allowed to hold such a licence. Special attention must also be paid to whether fatigue is experienced on the drugs. Full information regarding these licences may be obtained from *Medical Aspects of Fitness to Drive*, produced by the Medical Commission on Accident Prevention and published by HMSO.

22. Should a patient who is having regular blood pressure check-ups always have them done at the same time of day? Is there much diurnal variation?

During a row with his secretary a normotensive man's blood pressure might rise to 160/100, whereas at 4 a.m. it might be recorded at 50/0. A single reading, therefore, is difficult to interpret. Although there is a pattern to the diurnal variation of blood pressure it does not seem sensible to measure it at the same time on every occasion. A more representative indication of the overall BP situation of a patient will be obtained by recording at as many different times as possible. Do not forget to use the same arm each time, supported at heart level, the correct cuff size, the fifth phase and with the patient sitting.

It is a good idea to let patients with borderline hypertension check their own blood pressure for a limited period of time. I supply them with a portable, automatic, digital read-out sphygmomanometer and get them to take their BP about four times a day for two weeks. They are told to take their BP when relaxed, irritated, in bed and so on. At the end of two weeks one has an overall idea of the blood pressure and whether or not to treat. How accurate are these machines? Even though they may be somewhat variable, if enough measurements are taken the average will certainly give a figure good enough for any decision on treatment to be made .

23. A doctor tests the blood pressure of a man of sixty-seven. He blows up the cuff and obtains some systolic beats at 210. On deflating the cuff the beats disappear at 190, and re-start again on a regular basis at 160 to end in a diastolic of 95. Is this a common phenomenon? What is the explanation?

The 'auscultatory gap' is a common problem in taking blood pressure, although its mechanism is uncertain. If you inflate the cuff to greater than the systolic there will be no auscultatory sounds, as there is no flow of blood in the occluded artery. As the pressure is released, flow through the artery only occurs at the peak of the systolic, and the intermittent turbulence causes a tapping sound. As long as the cuff pressure exceeds diastolic there is interruption of flow, at least during some part of the cycle, allowing the tapping sound (Korotkoff sound) to continue. However, there is often a silent period as the sphygmomanometer pressure falls, presumably related to the turbulent sound being below the frequency level of hearing. This can be a problem because you may miss the 'top end' of the auscultatory sounds. To avoid this, the radial artery should be palpated as the cuff is inflated and a note made of the pressure at which the pulse disappears. The systolic pressure will then be confirmed correctly by auscultation. By convention, the diastolic pressure is the point *not* at which the sound changes, but at which it disappears entirely. That is to say, not at phase 4 but at phase 5.

Another source of error when taking blood pressure is using the the wrong size of cuff. Small cuffs should be used for children, and large cuffs should be used for patients with large arms. Using a normal size cuff on a fat arm will sometimes result in an alarming overestimate of the blood pressure.

Elderly Hypertension

24. What advice would you give to an elderly lady with moderately severe hypertension who wishes to fly to Canada on a family visit?

Being patriotic, the first piece of advice is, of course, to fly British Airways. However, flying on an aeroplane is the equivalent of being at an altitude of 5000 to 8000 feet. There is therefore no appreciable change in the partial pressure of oxygen whilst flying, and all heart patients, except those with the most severe congenital heart disease, are quite safe. The only circumstances which may change blood pressure are taking off and landing. These are known to increase the pilot's heart rate to about 140 per minute, let alone the passengers, and if the patient is very frightened, the blood pressure may rise too. A mild tranquilliser would probably solve this problem. It is also important to consider taking out adequate health insurance and sufficient tablets to cover emergencies such as aircraft delay. Generally, however, one has no hesitation in reassuring anyone in this situation. An elderly patient should be advised to take frequent short walks along the aisle to prevent a DVT.

25. You take an elderly man's blood pressure and find it raised. Before you do anything else you check his date of birth. Is there an age above which you would not treat hypertension?

Elderly hypertensives can be divided into three age groups: 60-69, 70-74, and 75 years and over. There is no particular medical reason for this except that the majority of trials have been conducted on the 60–69 age group and virtually none on those above 75. Although BP rises with age it does not apparently rise significantly in the older patient (Figure 9).

This has reinforced the view that because there is little rise we have to be very careful how vigorously we treat elderly hypertensives. In addition the Framingham study correlates hypertension and mortality very closely (Figure 10).

What is vital, however, is whether treatment makes any difference. The European working party on high blood pressure in the elderly suggests an improved morbidity, particularly with regard to strokes in the

60-69 age group. Small studies in the age group 70+ also suggest a small benefit in morbidity with treatment, but after the age of 75 the disadvantages of the treatment (see Question 26) probably outweigh the advantages.

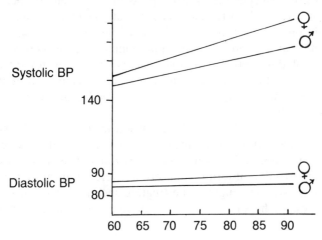

Figure 9   *Blood pressure change with age.*

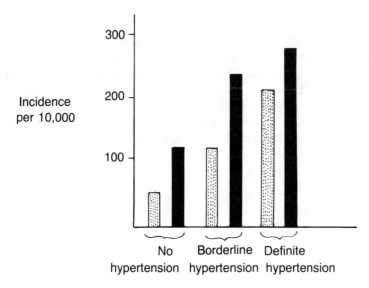

Figure 10   *Mortality rates in elderly hypertension.*

26. How would you treat a man of seventy with a BP of 200/80; and one with a BP of 250/80?

The presence of a wide pulse pressure (definition: systolic pressure minus diastolic pressure exceeds the diastolic pressure) in an elderly person is indicative of arteriosclerosis. This means that the blood vessels have become rigid pipes rather than flexible tubes. Impairment exists, therefore, of both baroreceptor activity and sympathetic responses. As a consequence of this, anti-hypertensive agents are poorly tolerated. In addition, renal function and drug pharmacokinetics behave differently in the elderly, so that there must be a very good indication to treat hypertension in this group.

The recent European Trial of Hypertension in the Elderly looked at patients with mild 'traditional' hypertension, i.e. raised systolic and diastolic (the mean blood pressure before treatment was approximately 180/100). In this trial, non-terminating strokes were significantly reduced, which has suggested we ought to be treating such patients, particularly those with 'systolic hypertension'. As a guideline, systolic hypertension would be:

Aged 70 — 180mmHg+
75 — 190mmHg+
80 — 200mmHg+

The practical problem is that systolic hypertension in the elderly is extremely difficult to treat. Either the drug has no effect at all or else it causes a precipitous and potentially dangerous fall in blood pressure. The rule is to try small doses of a wide variety of drugs – e.g. bendrofluazide 2.5mg, nifedipine either as 5mg t.d.s. or 10mg b.d. in its sustained-release form, and atenolol 50mg daily – one at a time. If there is no benefit it is quite reasonable to abandon attempts at treatment.

Exercise

27. What sport would you allow a man to play who is fifty years old and has had a myocardial infarction at the age of forty-six?

A formal treadmill test is essential before making any decision regarding exercise in a post-infarction patient. If this is positive, suggesting ischaemia, exercise must be limited and in the majority of cases angiography is appropriate. A positive exercise test may be associated with as high as a 27% one-year mortality rate. A negative exercise test suggests an almost normal one-year mortality rate – perhaps as low as 3%. Thus, if the treadmill test is negative, exercise is fine. Exercise should begin gently, as a matter of common sense, but in the United States some cardiac centres aim to enter their post-infarction patients for the Boston Marathon – after a suitable period of training. Ultimately, therefore, the sky is the limit, although prudence is vital, particularly in the case of squash, rowing, weight-training and similarly strenuous activities.

28. A man with known ischaemic heart disease exercises until he gets angina and then stops. Should he be advised to stop *before* he gets angina?

In typical angina pectoris, chest pain heralds the onset of ischaemia but not injury. Consequently a patient may quite safely exercise until he gets pain. There is evidence that regular exercise will increase the time to onset of angina, so that 'training' until pain is reached is valuable. Once pain has developed it is clearly necessary to stop exercise, otherwise severe ischaemia may precipitate an arrhythmia or even an infarction. Most patients learn to stop exercising at a certain level of pain or discomfort in the chest and can be reassured that they are doing themselves no harm.

23

29. A patient takes a large amount of exercise without any angina or distress. He complains however of a typically anginal pain being brought on by having an argument with his boss. Would a stress test based on exercise, e.g. treadmill, necessarily show evidence of coronary ischaemia? Is it less likely to do so under these conditions?

Coronary ischaemia should certainly be shown up in these circumstances. There can, however, be a significant number of false negative results in a standard treadmill test. There is a calculated heart rate – 90% of maximum according to age and sex – which should be reached if the test is to be valid. If this level is not reached, a diagnosis of ischaemic heart disease cannot be excluded with absolute certainty. For this reason the Masters two-step test is of little value, because by the time the patient lies down on the couch to have his ECG recorded the heart rate might already have dropped to 130.

When exercise is taken the majority of the increased heart action is chronotropism (i.e. increased heart rate), whereas a row with the boss stimulates a lot of inotropism as well (i.e. increased contraction of the left ventricle). However, the majority of patients, having been wired up and facing the treadmill, are somewhat apprehensive and so the test usually does combine chronotropism with inotropism quite well. In most cases, therefore, the treadmill test is very effective and is at present the best test we have. It must always be remembered that angina is a diagnosis based on the history and not on tests.

30. After what interval following exercise, e.g. squash, tennis, or running, should the pulse rate return to its resting level? How does this vary with age? What would you consider a significant prolongation of this interval, and how should it be investigated?

I do not think it is possible to answer this question with any certainty. The maximum heart rate achievable in a man is said to be 220 minus his age. Thus for a fifty-five year old man a maximum heart rate of 165 per minute should be possible. In those who are not athletes the theoretical rate to be aimed for is 70-85% of this maximum – a man of fifty-five should aim for 115-140 per minute.

Patients should be taught to take their pulse over a ten second period and gauge their own performance. Having achieved the target heart rate, they are advised to cool down whilst still exercising to a heart rate of about 100 and then stop. At this point the heart rate should fall by 7-9 beats per minute, so that it should be back to normal (say 70 per minute)

after about four minutes. If after six minutes the heart rate remains above
100-110 per minute, advice should be sought.

If you are faced with this problem in practice the patient must be
referred for an exercise test. Other signs are referred to in Question 34.

**31. A man who lives in a cottage some distance from the local shops has an
uncomplicated myocardial infarction. How long would it be before you
allowed him to drive a car short distances? Longer distances, for example
London to Cornwall? Should the driving licence authority be notified of a
myocardial infarction?**

The DVLC in Swansea recommends that a person should not drive a car
for eight weeks after a myocardial infarction, although this is not a legal
requirement. In many uncomplicated infarctions patients may well be
able to drive after as little as four weeks, although each case must be very
carefully assessed. Patients should increase their amount of driving
gradually, and it is certainly important not to drive long distances until
about eight weeks. Any driver who has had a myocardial infarction is
obliged to notify the DVLC.

**32. Does graduated exercise after a myocardial infarction improve prognosis,
or does it just increase exercise tolerance?**

There is no evidence, so far, that exercise either decreases or increases
the mortality rate or morbidity following a myocardial infarction.
Comparative studies have been complicated by the high drop-out rate in
the exercise groups. Intentions seem to be very good for about six months
after the heart attack but then rapidly tail off.

Is there *any* value in exercise after an infarction? It certainly increases
work capacity – less oxygen is required for the same amount of work.
The physiological reason for this seems to lie, not in increased myocardial
perfusion, but in the adaptation of peripheral musculature. Nevertheless,
this effect, in raising the threshold above which angina occurs, not only
improves both self-confidence and self-image, but also relieves anxiety
and depression.

Exercise groups do not seem to return to work any earlier but *do* tend
to adopt a healthier life style – stopping smoking, paying more attention
to diet, and so on. This can have the spin-off effect of improving blood
pressure.

A decent trial of exercise versus non-exercise in the post-infarction
patient is awaited with enthusiasm.

33. A cardiologist suggests a brisk walk of two miles a day as an ideal exercise. How brisk is brisk – i.e. what would be a reasonable completion time for the two miles?

Walking at 2 m.p.h. is regarded as very light exercise, 3-4 m.p.h. as light exercise, 4-5 m.p.h as moderate excercise and 5 m.p.h. or more (i.e. jogging) as heavy exercise. In a fifty year old man it would be reasonable to start with light exercise and proceed to moderate exercise but no further. Hence he should complete his brisk walk initially in 40 minutes, working up over six weeks to 25 minutes. This should be done about four times per week.

Jogging tends to increase the risk of orthopaedic injury and patients are much less likely to persevere. Walking at a moderate rate has been shown to increase the work capacity of the patient, and to decrease the fat content of the body as well as the weight. However, you will have to walk seventy miles non-stop to lose a pound of fat in one go!

34. A man of fifty insists on increasing the amount of exercise he takes. He asks you what might be the warning signs that he is 'overdoing it'. What would you say are the most significant?

Warning signs are important and I am constantly telling patients that they must not be ignored. If patients did take heed of these warnings, I am sure that some myocardial infarctions, and even a few sudden deaths, would be avoided.

Warning signs during exercise
These are fairly obvious. Angina, palpitations, lightheadedness, undue breathlessness and intermittent claudication all suggest cardiovascular disease until proved otherwise. Nausea is another possible sign, and if breathlessness persists for more than ten minutes after the exercise has stopped, suspicions should be aroused.

Warning signs following exercise
A most important sign is prolonged fatigue. Many patients complain of tiredness to an excessive degree in the run-up to a myocardial infarction. 'I can hardly hold up my arms, Doc.' Unusual insomnia occurring after exercise may be associated with 'just feeling terrible'. A persistent tachycardia may be significant. A heart rate in excess of 100 beats per minute, six minutes after exercise has ceased, is an adverse sign.

On the Safe Side

35. A man of fifty feels well. He is a non-smoker. He lives a healthy life. A routine medical examination for his employer shows a normal blood chemistry, but the ECG shows marked ischaemic changes. What action would you take, if any?

Marked ischaemic changes at rest must be regarded very seriously. If the changes (either ST segment depression or T wave inversion, or both) are due to ischaemia, the heart must be quite seriously affected. However, there are other causes of widespread T wave changes, such as hypertension, cardiomyopathies, myocarditis, hypothyroidism, digoxin therapy, hypokalaemia and bundle branch block.

One assumes that in such a medical examination the blood pressure has been measured, the serum T_3 has been checked and the patient has been asked about digoxin therapy. The most likely diagnoses lie between myocardial ischaemia and the various forms of cardiomyopathy, which includes myocarditis. Ischaemia is best diagnosed by an exercise test, cardiomyopathy by an echocardiograph. A patient with these ischaemic changes, therefore, even without any symptoms, must be referred to a specialist.

A word of warning. T waves are normally inverted in lead aVR and can be inverted as a normal variation in leads III, aVF and V_1. ST segments can be raised normally in leads V_{1-3}, especially in athletes and some Africans.

36. After a person has had a myocardial infarction from which they appear to have made a complete recovery, would you, at any stage, consider them to have an average expectation of life?

The main factors which predict survival after a myocardial infarction are age and size of infarction. It is impossible to generalise on survival, as everyone is slightly different. All of us will have heard of patients who have had a myocardial infarction in their forties and still remain in good health another forty years later.

An attempt was made to identify those at high risk after a myocardial

27

infarction by an exercise test, either submaximal seven to fourteen days after the event, or maximal six weeks after the event. There appeared to be quite a difference between those with positive tests and those with negative tests. The mortality at one year with a positive test has been as high as 27% while in a negative test it has been as low as 3%. Subsequent work has shown that it may not be absolutely necessary to do such a test. It may be equally useful simply to check for angina, heart failure or palpitations. If any of these are present the patient is in a high risk group and must be referred back to hospital for investigation.

If the patient is young, has had a small infarction and no subsequent symptoms, one can be encouraging about his life expectancy. It is probably not that different to the population at large. It would in addition depend on whether he was a non-smoker, whether he had hypertension and whether he had normal lipids. There are so many 'ifs' and 'buts' that a straight answer is impossible.

37. A man of fifty who feels well asks his doctor for an exercise tolerance test because he has been told it is a good idea for a man of his age to have one. Ideally, how should the doctor proceed?

The accuracy of defining which particular individual will have a future coronary event is poor, and is one of the reasons (or excuses) given for not bothering too much with preventative medicine. However, there is some evidence to suggest an exercise ECG might be of value. Professor G. Rose showed in his Whitehall Study that 14% of men who were positive either on questioning about symptoms or on a resting ECG generated 50% of the five-year cardiovascular deaths. Minor IHD, therefore, is a predictor of major IHD.

Would the exercise ECG be more valuable than a resting ECG? A study of over two thousand apparently healthy men showed that coronary events were significantly associated with abnormalities during an exercise test. The occurrence of chest pain, a low maximum work load, failure to reach 90% of the predicted maximal heart rate and changes in the ST segment all suggest the possibility of future cardiac events. Thus there is some evidence that an exercise test may be helpful, but it has to be balanced against cost and the anxiety produced if the test is positive. At present, cost is totally prohibitive, and under the NHS there is no chance of such a test on demand. It is fair to say to this 50-year old that there is no real evidence that an exercise test in these circumstances will be helpful, and that he has been incorrectly advised. (Not by you, of course!)

38. Another man comes and makes a similar request. He has no symptoms. His father died at fifty of a coronary, his brother at fifty-one. How should the doctor proceed?

This man has a high risk of ischaemic heart disease and is already frightened. The risk ratio in patients in the Framingham Study with first-degree relatives who have had IHD under the age of 55 years is 10.4 times normal, and is by far the biggest single risk factor. (Other figures for risk ratios are: cholesterol 7mmol/l = 4.3; smoking 10 cigarettes per day = 4.0; BP 160/100 = 1.8.) As the exercise test is the only non-invasive method of testing the function of a patient's heart which may be helpful, it is justified in sending this man to Outpatients for an exercise test, and if not already done, blood lipids.

39. A patient who has had by-pass surgery suffers, in the weeks following the operation, intermittent attacks of supraventricular tachycardia. Is this common? Is it of prognostic significance?

This is not an uncommon problem. It is due, presumably, to a mild inflammatory reaction around the atria. During operation, after a median sternotomy, the pericardium is opened to allow access to the heart. Because of this trauma, a mild pericarditis may result and produce atrial fibrillation for up to three months post-operatively.

Other atrial arrhythmias can occur, but it is usual to put a patient on regular digoxin to reduce the distress caused by the tachyarrhythmia. The arrhythmia has no prognostic significance, although the mild pericarditis can be part of the post-cardiotomy syndrome.

The post-cardiotomy syndrome is a widespread inflammatory reaction throughout the chest resulting in chest pain, dyspnoea, pericarditis, pleural effusion and fatigue. At its most severe it may last for up to two years. In mild cases, the syndrome may only last a few weeks. A non-steroidal anti-inflammatory drug such as indomethacin may be very beneficial.

40. A man of thirty-six is found to have a blood pressure of 150/90. His father died of a myocardial infarction at the age of forty-three. An elder brother of forty-four has already had one infarction. Would you suggest that this man should be given beta-blockers? Is there any evidence that taking a beta-blocker will reduce the incidence of coronary death?

One would be tempted to advise this gentleman not to join a Christmas Club. On face value he seems at considerable risk. He is male, borderline hypertensive with an obvious bad family history of ischaemic heart disease. But does it all add up?

His blood pressure is very borderline indeed. The MRC trial on hypertension taken with the American and Australian studies suggest very limited, if any, advantage in treating a patient with diastolic between 90-105. If there is evidence of end organ damage it would be worth treating a diastolic of 90, but otherwise not. A family history is always considered the major risk factor, and while this is undoubtedly true as a generalisation it is a poor individual prognosticator. Just because two members of this family have had a coronary does not mean the other members of the family will automatically be affected.

So, what do we do with this chap? The ideal thing here is an exercise test. If this shows any strain at all, with or without symptoms, a beta-blocker would be indicated. This is a case which, because of the risk factors, deserves referral to hospital for an exercise test as genuine preventative medicine. There is at present no evidence that beta-blockers are valuable in primary prevention, and in any case their side effects are not inconsiderable, particularly weariness and dreariness.

Medication

HEART FAILURE

41. A man with a history of myocardial ischaemia develops a mild degree of congestive cardiac failure. He has no arrhythmia. Under what circumstances would you prescribe digoxin?

Two relatively recent studies have suggested that digoxin increases mortality after a myocardial infarction. This is related to the fact that digoxin might cause lethal arrhythmias when the myocardium is already ischaemic, and has led to a renewed debate on its use in these circumstances.

Digoxin still remains extremely valuable when a patient has atrial fibrillation or similar supraventricular arrhythmia if the ventricular response rate is very fast, i.e. a heart rate of 130+. Its value in sinus rhythm remains debatable. Because of the question mark hanging over digoxin it is no longer used as first-line medication in mild congestive cardiac failure related to myocardial ischaemia. A diuretic is the treatment of choice unless there is a need to control atrial fibrillation. As the failure worsens the diuretic may be increased, and subsequently either digoxin or an ACE (angiotensin-converting enzyme) inhibitor, such as captopril, can be introduced.

42. Is there any reason not to give one diuretic, for example frusemide, in increasing doses rather than to give a mixed diuretic regime?

As heart failure worsens there is little option but to increase the diuretic. Increasing the dose of loop diuretics such as frusemide or butemanide makes hypokalaemia more likely. As a result there is an increased requirement for potassium supplement. Potassium is often slightly irritant to the gastric mucosa and can cause epigastric pain, even ulceration. In addition, a dose as high as eight tablets a day might be necessary. This is undesirable from the patient's point of view. As the need for diuretics increases, it is better to combine the loop diuretic with a potassium-conserving diuretic, e.g. amiloride or spironolactone. A combination of these diuretics, such as Frumil (frusemide and amiloride), may be very beneficial because less tablets are consumed. As a general rule, once 80mg or more of frusemide is required in a single dose, combination therapy should be considered. Do not forget to check urea and electrolytes after one month.

There are two other considerations. First, the combination of a loop diuretic with an ACE inhibitor is highly effective. ACE inhibitors not only act as vasodilators but also tend to restore electrolyte balance, in particular raising potassium levels already reduced by the loop diuretics. The development of ACE inhibitors has been one of the most significant advances in the treatment of heart failure for years. There is a tendency to think they cannot be used outside hospitals because a sudden drop in blood pressure may occur precipitously. This is true, but as a general rule they can be safely given if the systolic BP is 110 or above, as long as the diuretic dosage is halved when treatment starts. Thus a patient on 80mg of frusemide would be reduced to 40mg of frusemide when starting captopril. The starting dose of captopril would be 12.5mg b.d., working up to 25mg t.d.s.

The second alternative to increasing the dose of diuretics is to add metolazone, although one should watch out for dehydration. This has an additional diuretic action, which may be very effective. The dosage would be 10mg daily.

43. **A woman of seventy-five who lives alone has an attack of left ventricular failure in the night. There is no evidence of myocardial infarction. Are there any circumstances under which you would advise treatment other than intravenous diuretic? Are there any circumstances in which you would leave that patient alone in her own home?**

Undoubtedly intravenous diuretics are the treatment of choice for acute left ventricular failure, and I can see no other immediate alternative. Sitting the patient up and giving oxygen, if you have it, would complete the emergency treatment. There is no place for digoxin in this situation. Diamorphine, if used, has the added advantage of reducing the pulmonary artery pressure and thus the preload on the heart. Within half an hour it should be apparent whether or not the diuretic is going to clear the pulmonary oedema. If the patient remains extremely breathless admission to hospital is clearly essential. If the patient improves, the decision for admission in a lady of this age is probably social. She is going to feel pretty exhausted for a while after an acute attack of LVF, and unless there is adequate family support admission is inevitable.

Although there may be no obvious evidence of an infarction at the time of the attack, the enzymes are often found to be raised, indicating the LVF to be of ischaemic origin. However, even if the cause is a possible infarction, admission is not justified for that reason alone. There is no evidence that admitting a patient over the age of seventy with a myo-cardial infarction gives an improved life expectancy. In practical terms, the majority of patients with an acute attack of left ventricular failure will probably end up in hospital, simply because they will not be able to have adequate care at home. In addition, one must always bear in mind that LVF is not a diagnosis, and that the underlying cause must subsequently be determined.

ANTICOAGULANTS

14. Is there any indication for the use of anticoagulants in crescendo angina?

Although a few trials have suggested that some benefit may be gained by anticoagulating patients with crescendo or unstable angina, it is not yet routine to do so. Current hospital management is usually to give a beta-blocker, a calcium antagonist, a nitrate and aspirin with the patient on bed rest and being monitored. 85% will settle this way but 15% will proceed to urgent bypass grafting or angioplasty. This is a good operation with a mortality in these circumstances as low as 4%.

Unstable angina includes a number of syndromes characterised by severe chest pain at rest, proven by ECG to be ischaemia, but involving no actual myocardial damage. The pains may gradually build up, threatening an infarction (crescendo angina), but more usually they remain very variable over a few days, sometimes severe, sometimes mild, but still threatening an infarction (true unstable angina). Once the patient's pain has settled on medical treatment a decision has to be made as to whether angiography and possible operation is indicated. In practice, many will eventually come to operation following a very positive exercise test or further chest pain at rest despite treatment.

45. Is there any evidence that taking a small daily dose of salicylates is of benefit in any form of heart disease?

The ultimate cause of an artery becoming blocked is not known. It is thought to be related to the balance between prostacyclin, which dilates arterioles and prevents platelet aggregation, and thromboxane A_2, which constricts arterioles and promotes platelet aggregation. Any drug which reduces thromboxane A_2 might, therefore, be beneficial in the cardiovascular system for the prevention of both myocardial and cerebral infarction. Great interest has been aroused in the preventative value of aspirin, because it appears to influence the production of prostacyclin and thromboxane A_2. The chemical reaction producing these substances in the body is as follows:

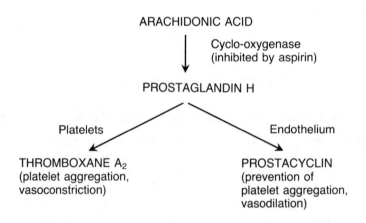

ARACHIDONIC ACID

Cyclo-oxygenase
(inhibited by aspirin)

PROSTAGLANDIN H

Platelets   Endothelium

THROMBOXANE A_2
(platelet aggregation,
vasoconstriction)

PROSTACYCLIN
(prevention of
platelet aggregation,
vasodilation)

As aspirin inhibits the production of both thromboxane *and* prostacyclin, is it really of much use? In fact it appears that thromboxane A_2 is the more sensitive to inhibition by aspirin. In any case, any reduction of thromboxane, whatever the level of prostacyclin, is of value. There is no evidence available in the case of primary prevention of heart disease but there have been six trials in the secondary prevention of myocardial infarction. Five of these trials showed a reduction of infarctions in the aspirin group compared with a placebo, but they were not statistically significant. The other trial showed neither benefit nor disadvantage.

Considering the trials as a whole, perhaps not altogether satisfactory but helpful, shows a reduction in recurrent myocardial infarction of 21% (P < 0.001, i.e. highly significant) and a reduction in cerebrovascular death of 16% (P < 0.01, i.e. significant).

The other question constantly asked is, 'What dose of aspirin?' It appears that dosages varying from 20mg to 325mg taken on a regular daily basis will inactivate more than 95% of the enzyme cyclo-oxygenase. Thus aspirin 300mg would be ideal, and is highly unlikely to have any adverse effect such as gastric irritation. On balance it would seem sensible to advise patients to take an enteric-coated aspirin a day, particularly for secondary prevention, because the advantages far outweigh the disadvantages.

46. A patient comes back from a holiday abroad where he has had a myocardial infarction. It is the policy of the doctors in that part of the world to treat myocardial infarction with anticoagulants. Would you continue the course, or tail it off rapidly, or slowly?

In 1970 the International Anticoagulant Review Group reported that, overall, there was a benefit from anticoagulants, but that more trials were needed. The only recent trial has been the 1980 60+ Reinfarction Study Research Group. Although this suggested benefit there were criticisms of the trial, and the incidence of bleeding problems in the anticoagulant group was significantly high.

Because of our current lack of knowledge regarding the benefit of anticoagulants, and the obvious disadvantages of bleeding, there is no indication for using them at present.

In hospital, low dose heparin (5,000 units b.d. or t.d.s.) is routinely and successfully used in post-myocardial infarction to prevent deep vein thrombosis, pulmonary emboli and mural thrombi. It is used only until the patient is mobile. In exceptional cases, anticoagulants might be continued e.g. in known left ventricular aneurysm, intermittent atrial fibrillation or low output syndrome. The patient referred to in this question should, therefore, have his anticoagulants stopped. They should be tailed off over a week.

47. In practice, which are the most common interactions that cause problems with warfarin?

A number of relatively common drugs interfere with warfarin metabolism. They can either make the patients more likely to bleed or they can prevent effective anticoagulation.

1) *Analgesics.* Aspirin, co-proxamol and the non-steroidal anti-inflammatory drugs may be used with extreme caution, but should be avoided if at all possible. All these will make the patient more likely to bleed. Codeine and the stronger opiates are safe. Paracetamol is also safe, unless given as regular treatment or in high doses.

2) *Antibiotics.* Sulphonamides (including co-trimoxazole), erythromycin and metronidazole increase the anticoagulant effect, whereas rifampicin, and to a certain degree griseofulvin, have the reverse effect. The penicillins and most of the cephalosporins are safe. (Check with BNF.)

3) *Antifungals.* Ketoconazole and miconazole enhance the anticoagulant effect.

4) *Sedatives.* Benzodiazepines like diazepam are safe. All barbiturates reduce the effectiveness of warfarin. Problems can arise in a patient who is taking barbiturates, when the dose of warfarin is adjusted to obtain a satisfactory prothrombin time. If the barbiturates are then stopped and the warfarin dosage is not reduced, haemorrhage can follow.

4) *Anticonvulsants.* Phenobarbitone, primidone and carbamazepine reduce the effect of warfarin. Sodium valproate (Epilim) is safe, but the effect of phenytoin is variable.

6) *Lipid-lowering agents.* Clofibrate and bezafibrate enhance warfarin action, and cholestyramine can interfere with warfarin control. Dextrothyroxine 'potentiates' the action of warfarin.

7) *Gastrointestinal agents.* Cimetidine increases the effect of warfarin, but ranitidine is safe.

8) *Endocrine drugs.* Anabolic steroids increase warfarin sensitivity, whereas oestrogens induce Vitamin K metabolism and have the opposite effect. If oral contraception is necessary whilst warfarin is being taken, a progesterone-only pill is the most appropriate.

9) *Others.* Amiodarone potentiates the action of warfarin quite markedly, and alcohol must be taken in moderation (no more than two or three units daily). Sulphinpyrazone also increases the action of warfarin. Steroids make gastrointestinal bleeding more likely, and are potentially dangerous with warfarin.

GENERALLY SAFE WITH WARFARIN:

Codeine   Strong opiates   Penicillins
Benzodiazepines   Ranitidine
Progesterone-only contraceptives
Paracetamol – see (1) opposite
Most cephalosporins – check with BNF

CARDIAC PAIN

48. What treatment should a GP give to a patient with a presumed myocardial infarction with bearable chest pain that is getting better? Bearable chest pain that is slowly getting worse? Crushing chest pain in a patient with a history of severe chronic obstructive airways disease?

At present there is no treatment available for the myocardial infarction itself. All treatment is either for the symptoms or for any complications that might follow. Chest pain which is improving probably requires no treatment at all, although I would personally give diamorphine anyway to cheer the patient up after his awful ordeal.

Chest pain which is getting worse is worrying, because continuous chest pain is a bad prognostic sign. Although diamorphine is helpful and must be given, it should be followed by a nitrate infusion. Intravenous nitrates are extremely useful in the vasodilation of both coronary and peripheral arteries in this critical situation and they *might* limit infarction size. They can prevent the need for repeated IV diamorphine. Such an infusion must be given in hospital so that careful monitoring of blood pressure, and if necessary central venous pressure, can take place.

In a patient with severe chronic obstructive airways disease, diamorphine or any of the opiate analogues will depress respiration and are contraindicated. Pentazocine, which does not depress respiration, raises the pulmonary artery pressure, increasing the workload of the heart. It should be avoided if at all possible. In cases of severe COAD one should give dihydrocodeine, but if this is not strong enough pentazocine or similar must be used. Because many smokers – who by the very nature of things can be considered to have a degree of COAD – suffer myocardial infarction, the use of opiates depends on each individual case. They clearly should not be used in a man on continuous oxygen or who is usually cyanosed at rest. They can be used in a man who has nothing more than a smoker's morning cough.

49. Ambulancemen often give nitrous oxide/air mixture to patients with myocardial infarction. Is this a dangerous practice?

The only haemodynamic effect of nitrous oxide and oxygen is moderate vasodilatation. This in turn stimulates the baroreceptors, causing a modest increase in both the heart rate and the cardiac output. As this is all at the expense of increased oxygen demand by the heart, the value of the gaseous mixture could be questioned. However, its usefulness in relieving pain, with the haemodynamic benefit that results, usually outweighs any adverse effect of the nitrous oxide itself. The giving of nitrous oxide/oxygen mixture in myocardial infarction is widespread and appears to be perfectly safe.

It is worth saying that if you think your patient has had a myocardial infarction, adequate analgesia given immediately, before the ambulance arrives, is the best idea. Intravenous diamorphine 5mg mixed in the same syringe with prochlorperazine 12.5mg would be very much appreciated. Another analgesic/anti-emetic mixture such as Cyclimorph could also be used. Contraindications would be chronic obstructive airways disease (see Question 48) or a situation such as the patient being on a monoamine oxidase inhibitor. It is, of course, essential that the admitting doctors know exactly what has been given and when.

When administering morphine, naloxone should be available for the very occasional respiratory arrest. Naloxone is short-acting and may need repeating.

50. A patient with moderate angina refuses to take a long-acting mononitrate, saying that he prefers to use glyceryl trinitrate. He takes up to eight a day. Symptoms apart, is this more harmful to his myocardium?

No. Angina pectoris is a warning sign, not evidence of myocardial damage occurring. If one does not heed the warning injury could occur, but if the patient is sensible, intermittent GTN is as appropriate as a long-acting mononitrate.

Long-acting mononitrates were developed because the dinitrates are largely inactivated by the liver, and in theory last no longer than GTN. Mononitrates may genuinely last much longer (as with the buccal or patch dinitrates). There is no doubt that some patients benefit considerably from long-acting nitrates, although present evidence suggests that tachyphylaxis – the rapidly declining response to a drug after administration of a few doses – soon arises if there is no break during the 24-hours cycle.

51. By what mechanisms are coronary vasodilator patches applied to the chest wall supposed to work? Do they in fact work? Why are they used so much more in the United States than in the United Kingdom?

At present there is only one type of vasodilator patch – the nitrate patch. Nitrate is absorbed from these patches transdermally, giving a peak level in the blood stream at six hours. Each patch may last twenty-four hours. The advantage is that there is prolonged action. Oral mononitrates peak at one to two hours and need to be taken three times per day.

Why their use is less common in the UK than in the USA and other countries, e.g. Germany, is difficult to explain. Our primary approach to angina is beta-blockers. In Germany it is a nitrate. No one is right or wrong, but it does emphasise that there is some value in nitrates and perhaps we should use them rather more.

ARRHYTHMIAS

52. Would you give intravenous beta-blockers under any circumstances in an emergency situation where the benefit of ECG monitoring was not available?

In the post-infarction situation, intravenous beta-blockers have been used, enthusiastically, in the belief that they might improve prognosis by decreasing infarction size. The question is – do they improve the chance of survival?

In the year following an infarction, beta-blockers do seem to improve the prognosis, but there is no absolute need, at any stage, for them to be given intravenously. Indeed, beta-blockers, by this route, carry a risk of provoking left ventricular failure, and the practice is no longer popular.

The evidence supporting the use of beta-blockers in the first year following a myocardial infarction comes from the pooled data of a large number of trials. The mortality rate at the end of one year, in those patients given a placebo, is 10.2%. In those taking beta-blockers it is 7.5% – a 26% reduction. (The total number of infarctions per annum in the UK is 200,000 +.)

Although it is hard to argue against these facts, permanent therapy is a constant reminder to the patient of the serious illness he or she has suffered. The best compromise, if it is possible, is to put those patients who have a positive exercise test six weeks post infarction on to beta-blockers, but to leave those patients who have had a negative exercise test well alone.

53. Would you give intravenous atropine in any emergency situation where the benefit of ECG monitoring was not available?

Atropine is one of the intravenous drugs well worth keeping in the emergency bag for use in myocardial infarctions or vasovagal attacks.

After a myocardial infarction a patient may look grey and sweaty, have a low blood pressure and appear to be in a state of collapse. It is not necessarily cardiogenic shock. It could be a vasovagal reaction. Atropine can be dramatically effective in these circumstances.

The most important indication for using atropine is a slow heart rate. It is not always easy to feel a very slow pulse of perhaps 30-35 per minute, and it might only be detected by auscultation. Even if the bradycardia is the result of complete heart block, atropine will do no harm and is worth giving. Although it is true that atropine may change 2:1 block to complete heart block, this is of no great practical importance.

In normal circumstances the dose of atropine is 0.6mg (one phial) given intravenously. It is important to remember, however, that if a vasovagal attack has occurred in a patient already taking a beta-blocker, a larger dose may be necessary. In hospital we sometimes give as much as 2.4mg (four phials), but it might be more appropriate for a doctor in a GP situation to consider urgent admission if two phials have not worked.

54. Is there still a place for using quinidine, either by itself or with other medication in the treatment of supraventricular tachycardia?

Quinidine is still considered to be an effective drug for the treatment of supraventricular arrhythmias, but it is limited in its use by a reputation for causing lethal arrhythmias, particularly ventricular tachycardia. The therapeutic blood levels and toxic blood levels are simply too close. Slow-release quinidine (Kinidin Durules) has much less toxicity and is given twice daily. However, quinidine in any form has gone out of favour and the 'Top 3' drugs for supraventricular tachycardia are: verapamil, amiodarone and disopyramide. (Others are beta-blockers, quinidine and digoxin.)

Verapamil is the drug of choice (except in heart failure) because it has a high chance of success and its only common side effect is constipation. *It is very important, however, that verapamil is never given with a beta-blocker.* It may cause asystole.

Amiodarone is highly effective. Unfortunately it has a number of side effects (see Question 57).

Disopyramide was launched as the modern-day quinidine. It is very efficient but, once again, there are troublesome side effects – notably dry mouth, urinary retention (particularly in the elderly), cerebellar disturbance and blurred vision.

Beta-blockers are of most value in the treatment of arrhythmias such as ectopics and 'heavy thumping of the heart', which appear to be caused by excessive catecholamine release. The top three drugs for ventricular arrhythmias in the long term are: flecainide, mexiletine and tocainamide. Lignocaine is used by the intravenous route *only*.

HYPERTENSION

55. A man of forty-four has moderate hypertension. He is started on a dose of atenolol 100mg daily. How soon after being seen should he be checked again, to make sure that he has not developed a significant bradycardia? Do many patients rapidly develop an unacceptable degree of bradycardia?

Although a beta-blocker will cause a bradycardia there is no need to be concerned unless tha patient has symptoms. The pulse will often drop to 48-50 per minute, but with no evidence of lightheadedness or syncope. It is not therefore necessary to call a patient back to the surgery just to check his pulse. The pulse will fall quite markedly on atenolol 50mg, often to about 50 per minute, but if the blood pressure demands an increase of the atenolol to 100mg it does not mean that the pulse will fall even more. Once the patient is fully 'beta-blocked' it does not matter how much more beta-blocker is given – the pulse rate will not fall any further; nor, most likely, will the blood pressure! It is important to remember, however, that patients who are fully beta-blocked are prone to occasional fainting from extreme bradycardia with less stimulation than would normally be required, e.g. intubation at operation.

Nevertheless, as a general rule, it is the symptoms that are relevant and not the pulse rate.

56. A man of fifty-eight has been taking methyldopa for fourteen years. His blood pressure is well controlled and he feels no ill effects. Should he be changed to a 'Modern Hypotensive'? What are the indications for using methyldopa?

No. He does not need to change his medication. There is nothing wrong with methyldopa. It is a good antihypertensive in certain individuals, and unless there are troublesome side effects there is no point in changing to another antihypertensive. The side effects of methyldopa are sleepiness, postural hypotension, impotence in males, and occasionally a haemolytic anaemia. They are not uncommon, and if one traces back over the last twenty years it is clear that the 'best buy' antihypertensive is basically the one with the least side effects.

FAVOURED HYPOTENSIVE:

1970	1975	1980
diuretics	diuretics	diuretics
methyldopa	propranolol	beta-blocker
bethanidine	methyldopa	nifedipine

1985	1990(?)	
nifedipine	nifedipine	
beta-blocker	ACE inhibitor	=
diuretics	beta-blocker/	
	diuretics	

MISCELLANEOUS

57. Under what circumstances should one consider using: 1) amiodarone? 2) xamoterol? 3) enalapril/captopril?

Amiodarone. Named the 'Domestos of Antiarrhythmic Drugs' by Professor John Camm, amiodarone is highly successful in 'killing all known supraventricular arrhythmias'. It is easily the best drug available for such arrhythmias as atrial fibrillation, supraventricular tachycardia and atrial tachycardia with variable block. It is not quite so successful for ventricular arrhythmias. I see no reason why it cannot be used in general practice, but there are side effects of which the doctor should be aware.

Some papers report as many as 70% of patients developing a light-sensitivity skin rash, often quite devastating. Just a minute in the sun and the skin can become hot, painful and red. In some patients the skin becomes a slate-grey colour. Pulmonary fibrosis has been reported. Amiodarone interferes with thyroid function tests and prolongs the prothrombin time, sometimes fatally, in patients on warfarin. It is not therefore recommended as a first-line agent, and is officially for refractory arrhythmias. My own experience, however, is that it can transform a patient's life, and in resistant cases is well worth trying.

Xamoterol. This drug, not yet on the open market, is the 'new digoxin'. It is a 'positive inotrope/negative chronotrope'. It makes the ventricle contract more strongly but prevents the heart rate exceeding about 120 per minute. This is because it is a beta agonist/antagonist. It is used in mild to moderate heart failure, often with much success. It can be used with digoxin or any other anti-failure therapy. Most of the newer inotropic agents have been criticised because they appear to drive the heart too hard and may precipitate sudden death. Xamoterol has a braking effect on the heart rate, which may prevent this happening.

Enalapril/captopril. These are ACE inhibitors. They prevent the production of angiotensin II, thus being of use in both hypertension and heart failure. This class of drug is well worth using because of its relatively few side effects. It is valuable in the treatment of heart failure not only because it acts as a vasodilator, but also because it tends to correct any electrolyte imbalance. In hypertension it may be used alone or in conjunction with a potassium-losing diuretic, e.g. bendrofluazide or frusemide. The use of a potassium-retaining diuretic is contraindicated, because it may create excessive hyperkalaemia. Almost any level of hypertension from mild upwards will benefit. In heart failure there may be a drop in blood pressure, so it should only be used if the systolic blood pressure is 110+, and then initially only with the smallest dose available.

58. It is inadvisable to give beta-blockers to a patient with bronchospasm. What medication would you consider inadvisable to use in a patient with bronchospasm who is also known to have ischaemic heart disease?

All beta-blockers are contraindicated in any patient with any form of bronchospasm. This includes any combination tablet which contains a beta-blocker, e.g. with a diuretic or a calcium antagonist, as well as beta-blocker eyedrops.

Bronchospasm is treated by a number of drugs which may affect the cardiovascular system. Salbutamol, terbutaline, pirbuterol, reproterol and rimiterol are, basically, modified isoprenalines and cause a weak cardiac excitation, but they will rarely, if ever, exacerbate angina. Indeed, they may relieve it by bronchodilation and by increasing the oxygen saturation. Inhalation of these drugs is preferable to oral administration because it enables lower doses to be used, giving less tachycardia and tremor. In general, they are perfectly safe in ischaemic heart disease.

Aminophylline is occasionally given intravenously in an emergency situation. It is a cardiac stimulant and must be given with great care, i.e. very slowly or not at all, in patients with ischaemic heart disease. Theophylline orally or aminophylline suppositories are relatively safe, because their serum concentrations are much less than IV aminophylline.

Prednisone could be contraindicated in ischaemic heart disease complicated by heart failure because it causes sodium and water retention. However, it can be of the most dramatic benefit in asthma, so a balance has to be struck. Because the sodium and water retention can be easily controlled by increasing the diuretic dosage, the balance is in favour of using prednisone in managing severe bronchospasm.

Smoking, Sex, Spirits, Sun and Sauna

59. Would you consider that a man of seventy, who has had two myocardial infarctions in the past five years, would have a significantly higher expectation of life if he were to give up the ten cigarettes a day that he has habitually smoked since the age of fifteen?

A number of studies in the last two years have demonstrated that those who continue to smoke more than five cigarettes per day after a myocardial infarction have about twice the mortality risk of those who cease to smoke. There is even a suggestion that passive smoking may increase the risk; in theory, everyone should be urged to stop smoking.

After two myocardial infarctions at the age of seventy the answer becomes more philosophical. It is doubtful whether a patient would live for *years* longer, and he might not want to anyway. In circumstances such as this, smoking can be a major source of pleasure and so much part of a patient's life that he may feel utterly miserable if he has to stop.

It is our job as doctors to advise a patient, not to tell him what to do. There is no point in getting cross, particularly with a man of this age, if he continues to smoke. If the patient has angina this can be increased by smoking, in which case there may be a genuine improvement in the quality of life when he stops. It would certainly be wrong to dictate to the patient in this question.

60. A patient with known ischaemic heart disease is going on holiday. Is there any hazard from sunbathing? Or from taking a sauna?

Sunbathing and hot showers produce some peripheral vasodilation, whereas saunas produce it to a very considerable degree. Sunbathing is unlikely to be a hazard unless sunstroke occurs, so the advice is simply to be careful and not overdo it. Hot showers can be a problem after exercise unless there has been a cooling-off period of about twenty minutes. Saunas are a different matter. Diverting blood to the periphery may significantly deprive the central circulation. If a significant degree of ischaemic heart disease is present, having a sauna may result in a rapid fall in blood pressure and possible serious cardiac arrhythmias.

61. Does the benefit of moderate drinking e.g. 4 units a day (one unit being a single spirit, a glass of wine or a half pint of beer) outweigh the disadvantages in a man of fifty with known ischaemic heart disease?

Epidemiological studies are split equally between those showing that alcohol is beneficial and those demonstrating deleterious effects, e.g. the accelerated atherosclerosis and cardiomyopathy that can follow heavy alcohol consumption. Modest consumption of alcohol raises the HDL cholesterol, which is possibly beneficial, but even small doses of alcohol can be negatively inotropic during exercise. Moderate consumption of alcohol may raise blood pressure, which is readily reversible on cessation of drinking. Overall it seems reasonable to allow a man with ischaemic heart disease to drink 4 units of alcohol per day.

62. It is often said that sex with one's usual partner is not contraindicated following a myocardial infarction. Is this a tongue-in-cheek way of saying that the experience should not be too exciting? If so, should you advise a man in similar circumstances not to go to Wembley if his team are playing in the Cup Final? Is 'excitement' a hazard for the post-infarction patient? And if so, for how long?

As a general rule one can resume sexual intercourse with one's regular partner about three to four weeks after a myocardial infarction. With a regular partner it is said that, on average, the sexual act takes place twice a week, lasts 16 minutes and results, hopefully, in an orgasm lasting 15 seconds. This is the physical equivalent of walking about half a mile, followed by climbing two flights of stairs. With an occasional partner the effect may be much more considerable, ending up with perhaps five or six flights of stairs. Such excitement is best avoided until about eight weeks post myocardial infarction, and preferably after a negative exercise test.

In theory, a myocardial infarction is healed after six weeks and all normal activities can continue from then on, including watching the Cup Final. If faced with the problem of a man six weeks post-infarction who wishes to get excited in this, or any other manner, three questions must be asked. Does he have chest pain? Does he get unduly breathless? Does he have palpitations or lightheadedness? Evidence of angina, heart failure or significant arrhythmias should preclude any 'excitement' until appropriate treatment, either medical or surgical, has been instituted.

63. Smoking is always mentioned as a risk factor in cardiovascular disease. In respiratory disease it seems that pipe smoking is not considered as hazardous as cigarette smoking. Does the same criterion apply to smoking and cardiovascular disease?

Most studies show little increased risk from either cigar or pipe smoking in cardiovascular disease as long as the smoking is considered 'light'. Heavy pipe and cigar smokers certainly have an increased risk of cardiovascular disease, although not as much as cigarette smokers. Nicotine in alkaline cigar smoke can be absorbed in the mouth, whereas the more acid cigarette smoke can only be absorbed in the lungs. This suggests that cigar smokers are more likely to inhale less because they can get their nicotine 'fix' more easily.

Do cigarette smokers who switch to cigars or pipe smoking reduce their risk? Although there is no evidence on this point it seems a logical conclusion that they would, although the best advice is to give up smoking altogether. One of the problems facing cigarette smokers who switch to pipes or cigars is that they are likely to inhale more, reducing their risk only slightly. It must also be remembered that pipe and cigar smoking does increase the risk of cancer of the mouth, throat, oesophagus and lungs above that of non-smokers. Cigarette smokers run the risk of a 50-100% greater death rate from all causes than non-smokers. Cigar and pipe smoking risk runs at 1-20%

Surgery

64. A man of fifty-five needs a non-urgent operation requiring a general anaesthetic. How long after an uncomplicated myocardial infarction would you allow him to have this?

The risk of reinfarction and death is not inconsiderable if elective surgery is performed too soon after a myocardial infarction. The overall reinfarction rate is about 18%, of whom 50% may die. The infarction rate in patients with no history of ischaemic heart disease is 0.1%. The reinfarction risk is highest in the first month after a myocardial infarction (approximately 37%), dropping to 4.5% at six months. With these figures in mind it is sensible to wait three months, and preferably six months, before operating.

In each individual case there is a balance between the need for the operation and the reinfarction risk. Two important factors are part of this equation. First, there is a greater risk in operations involving the thorax and upper abdomen compared with the lower abdomen. Secondly, an operation likely to produce hypotension carries a significantly higher risk. Every operation has its own mortality rate, and the risk of death from reinfarction must be added to this.

65. Is there any age above which you would *not* consider a patient, otherwise fit, for coronary by-pass surgery or aortic valve surgery?

There are no absolute rules about age prohibiting major heart operations, but biological age is more important than chronological age. Some sixty-year olds look seventy-five, and vice versa. It is wrong, in my opinion, for any unit to adopt an upper age limit because of restriction of funds, etc. – each case depends on an individual assessment.

Perhaps the most important factor in successfully surviving heart surgery is the state of the left ventricle. If this is poor before the operation, mortality and morbidity will be high. Inevitably the left ventricular function worsens with the length of time the patient has suffered from his condition. A patient who first develops symptoms from his mitral incompetence at the age of sixty will be, at sixty-five, a better candidate than a man of the same age who has had the symptoms for twenty years.

In ischaemic heart disease the left ventricle is frequently damaged, and as a general rule few coronary artery bypass operations will be carried out after the age of seventy-five years. A similar situation exists in aortic incompetence and mitral valve disease. Aortic stenosis is different because there is often little impairment of the left ventricle until a very late stage and excellent results can be obtained up to eighty years or more.

66. What evidence is there to suggest that bypass surgery increases life expectancy?

Coronary artery bypass surgery is primarily for pain. However, in two situations life expectancy is increased. The coronary arteries are like the fingers of the left hand. The thumb represents the right coronary artery going along the inferior aspect of the heart. The first finger is the left anterior descending coronary artery, and the middle finger is the circumflex artery, which goes laterally round the heart (Figure 11).

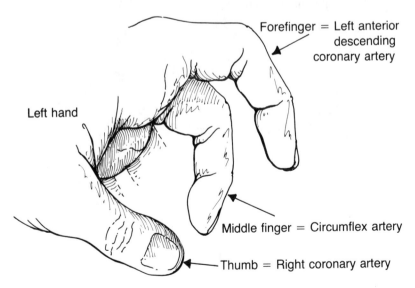

Forefinger = Left anterior descending coronary artery

Left hand

Middle finger = Circumflex artery

Thumb = Right coronary artery

Figure 11   *Demonstration of the coronary arteries.*

Left main stem disease is classically known as the 'widow maker'. The 5-year survival medically is 60%, but surgically it is 90%. This is an enormous difference. The other condition in which surgery confers a prognostic advantage is triple vessel disease. If all three vessels are involved, the 5-year survival, medically treated, is 80% and surgically treated, is 90%.

One's immediate reaction to these figures is that everyone with angina should have angiography. This is not possible in present circumstances, but an exercise test can be very helpful. In such a test, left main stem disease can be suspected if the ST segments drop very quickly, e.g. at a heart rate of less than 100 per minute, or if there is a marked drop in blood pressure during exercise, e.g. from 180/90 to 100/60 (Figure 12).

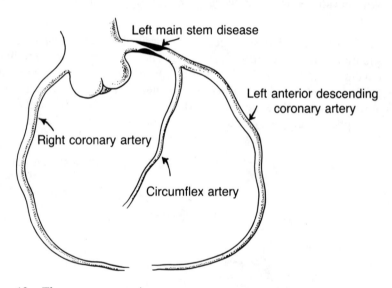

Figure 12   *The coronary arteries.*

67. A man of forty-seven has bypass surgery for triple artery disease. He is a cheerful individual and never makes a fuss. His wife visits him a few days post-operatively and is most distressed to find him in tears. Is such depression, following cardiac surgery, a common event?

It is a very common event in the first three or four weeks after any heart operation, but may last seven to ten days. It rarely needs treating. There is an emotionally exhausting build-up to any major operation, but because of the heart's status as *the* vital organ, it applies to cardiac surgery in particular. The post-operative depression could well be explained as a reaction to this kind of exhaustion. There might, however, be a more complex and physical reason.

70% of post-operative patients are reported as having some neurological deficit for a period after the operation, although in the vast majority it is exceedingly minor, e.g. a transient upgoing plantar reflex. The depression may therefore be due to the bypass procedure itself, or perhaps from hypotension or microemboli. The treatment of the depression is first to warn the patient pre-operatively that it might occur, and then to reassure the patient during his crisis that he will rapidly improve. Drugs are rarely, if ever, needed.

68. What is the five-year survival rate for patients with triple bypass surgery?

90% . It is important to remember that the survival rate for medically-treated triple vessel disease is 80% (see Question 66), provided that the left ventricular function is normal or near normal.

Arrhythmias

69. How long would you allow an attack of supraventricular tachycardia to go on, untreated, in a child of 10? A man of 25? A man of 60?

There are two indications for treating an arrhythmia: i) if it is inherently dangerous, e.g. ventricular tachycardia; and ii) if it has caused, or is likely to cause, left ventricular failure. Thus, atrial ectopics, which are neither inherently dangerous nor likely to cause left ventricular failure need not be treated on medical grounds. They may, of course, need treatment on symptomatic grounds.

A supraventricular tachycardia is not inherently dangerous, i.e. it will not by itself lead to a cardiac arrest. However, because its rate is usually 170+ per minute, it will increase the risk of left ventricular failure, particularly in the presence of underlying ischaemic or other form of heart disease. A child of ten and man of twenty-five are unlikely to have an underlying heart disease, so one would not be unduly concerned about them. A man of sixty is likely to have some sort of acquired heart disease and is very likely to go into left ventricular failure at some stage.

Unless the child of ten or man of twenty-five is distressed by the tachycardia, there is plenty of time to consider action – i.e. days. You would not leave someone having an SVT for life, and so eventually something must be done, but there is no rush. They can be safely sent to Casualty or a cardiac clinic the next day unless they become panic-stricken, in which case giving a tranquilliser is quite permissible. The man of sixty needs urgent hospital admission, i.e. within 1-2 hours, because it is most likely that he has ischaemic heart disease, perhaps even a recent myocardial infarction, and will go into failure if not treated.

70. If you decided on immediate treatment of a tachycardia, and a cardiograph was not available, what action would you take?

I think the only action one can take is to stimulate the vagus nerve and if this fails, as it usually does, to refer the patient to the local Casualty. This is not an admission of failure, because it is very important to characterise the tachycardia if at all possible by recording it on an ECG. It could be supraventricular tachycardia, atrial tachycardia, ventricular tachycardia, junctional tachycardia, atrial fibrillation, atrial tachycardia with varying block and so on.

These attacks are often recurrent, so an accurate diagnosis is very useful for the future. Stimulating the vagus nerve will only stop an attack of supraventricular tachycardia, a generally benign condition. This in itself is a useful diagnostic tool. It rarely has a long-lasting effect and the tachycardia often recurs after a few minutes, at which point the patient can, perhaps, be sent for an ECG. Nevertheless, successful stimulation of the vagus nerve is encouraging to the patient at the time, it is diagnostically useful, and is something the patient can learn to do for himself in dealing with future attacks. The usual means of stimulating the vagus nerve at the bedside are: i) rubbing the carotid vessels one at a time; and ii) pressing the eyeballs. These rarely work, because it is difficult to get at the vagus nerve (which is situated *behind* the carotid), and because the eyeball method is only successful if you virtually enucleate the eye. Neither procedure is easy for the patient to do for himself on future occasions.

More successful from the patient's point of view are other methods, such as:

1) Rapidly drinking a glass of very cold water. A bottle of cold water can be kept in the fridge for the occasion, next to the champagne to be drunk if the treatment is successful, as it may well be.
2) Making oneself sick. This is a highly successful, if perhaps socially unacceptable method.
3) Plunging one's face into a washing-up bowl of cold water. This is not too pleasant and one can imagine the elderly patient drowning himself.
4) Carrying out the Valsalva manoeuvre. It is very difficult to explain to patients how to expire forcibly against a closed glottis. I think the best method is to tell them to blow up a balloon. Even if it bursts, the fright of it doing so might curtail the tachycardia.

71. Under what circumstances can a person with a pacemaker go into sudden cardiac arrest? Can a defibrillator be used on someone with a pacemaker?

It would be nice to be able to tell a patient that now that they have a pacemaker their heart can never stop. However, such patients may have pacemaker failure and are as prone to cardiac arrest as any other equivalent member of the population. Cardiac arrest occurs with:

1) Ventricular fibrillation.
2) Asystole.
3) Complete heart block with Stokes-Adams attack (see Question 73).

If the pacemaker battery fails, the mechanism breaks down, the pacemaker wire breaks, or the tip of the electrode becomes dislodged from the right ventricle, problems (2) and (3) can occur and need to be treated urgently with a replacement pacemaker system. This can be done very quickly with a temporary pacing wire and box under X-ray control. Nothing can be done on the spot to the existing pacemaker system, so normal cardiopulmonary resuscitation should be started until the patient reaches the hospital and the X-ray department.

Ventricular fibrillation is caused by a wide variety of underlying heart conditions and stimuli which are quite independent of the pacemaker. Defibrillation is quite safe as the pacemaker has a cut-off protective mechanism.

In practice, patients with faulty pacemaker systems will have transient lightheadedness or blackouts rather than a full-blown cardiac arrest, and such symptoms demand that the system is checked by the hospital within the week.

72. When people appear to drop dead from a myocardial infarction it is said that most of them are in ventricular fibrillation and not in a state of true arrest. If this was generally the case, would not the availability of a cheap, easy-to-use defibrillator for stimulation of an apparently arrested individual, even *without* ECG monitoring, save a substantial number of lives?

The answer is 'yes', as long as you reach the patient in time. The majority of cardiac arrests are ventricular fibrillation and, in any case, a defibrillation shock is unlikely to do any harm to the patient with asystole. Defibrillation is rarely successful unless the heart is reasonably oxygenated, and since a doctor is unlikely to be standing over a patient when he arrests, except perhaps in hospital, it will always be difficult to save a substantial number of lives.

If the entire population could perform cardiopulmonary resuscitation until a defibrillator was available, there might be some hope. This has been done in Seattle, USA, and is considered at least partially successful, but it would be an overwhelming burden for someone to organise in the UK. Douglas Chamberlain and his colleagues have shown great enthusiasm in setting this up in Brighton and are much to be congratulated, but such a service is unlikely to be universally available. In this type of project it is usually the ambulancemen or paramedics who defibrillate, often with considerable skill. Because they are available through the '999' system, they may be more likely to be at the scene of an arrest before the GP. Nonetheless, there is a good argument that a GP should have a defibrillator.

If a cheap, easy-to-use, portable, rechargeable defibrillator was available, I would have no hesitation in recommending its use on the pulseless patient.

73. Is there a degree of bradycardia above which one might safely assume a patient is not in imminent danger of Stokes-Adams attack? Is there a pulse rate below which you would consider such attacks imminent, and require the patient to be immediately hospitalised?

Stokes-Adams or drop attacks involve sudden loss of consciousness without any warning whatsoever. The patient is completely alright one minute, and falls to the floor as if dead the next. Injuries, particularly to the face, are very common. They occur in both complete heart block and the sick sinus syndrome. In neither case is there any warning sign of an impending attack, whether from signs or symptoms or the ECG. Therefore, whatever the heart rate, you must assume that once a diagnosis of complete heart block or sick sinus syndrome is made, a Stokes-Adams or drop attack is always a possibility. The sick sinus syndrome is a condition which manifests itself as a variety of both bradycardias and tachycardias causing dizziness, lightheadedness and occasionally Stokes-Adams attacks.

The only treatment for these conditions is a pacemaker. Implanting a pacemaker is so easy, so reliable and so effective that there are no contraindications, except congenital complete heart block. In this condition Stokes-Adams attacks are very rare indeed, and the patient compensates for his rate problem from birth so well, that a pacemaker is rarely necessary.

In the elderly patient a slow pulse brings the added complication of heart failure, even if Stokes-Adams or drop attacks do not occur. A rate below 50 per minute must be highly suspect. Even if heart failure is not present when the patient is first seen, it will inevitably ensue as the patient grows older. As a general rule, anyone with a pulse rate of less then 45 per minute ought to have an ECG.

74. Is it true that a bradycardia following a myocardial infarction is a more likely precursor of ventricular fibrillation than a degree of tachycardia?

No. Ventricular fibrillation is probably related to the degree of myocardial ischaemia, which in turn can be made more critical as much by a bradycardia as a tachycardia. In the majority of cases tachycardias are less well tolerated than bradycardias, and a ventricular tachycardia may lead to a ventricular fibrillation as a result of the electrical interference. Ventricular ectopics were once thought to be precursors of ventricular fibrillation. This is not necessarily so. There is no way of predicting which type of ventricular ectopic is more dangerous than another (although the R on T phenomenon still carries an increased risk).

75. A man with an athletic bradycardia of 48 beats per minute is unfortunate enough to have a myocardial infarction. Is he more at risk from a dangerous bradycardia than someone with a normal resting pulse rate?

No. In fact he is possibly at less risk if he does develop a dangerous bradycardia.

An athletic bradycardia occurs because the peripheral vasculature adapts and the stroke volume increases. There is more 'reserve' in the heart to cope with stress. Unless an infarction is large, the athletic patient is more likely to compensate for a bradycardia than an unfit patient, because of the increased stroke volume. The existence of a bradycardia before an infarction is in no way related to that which may occur after an infarction. After an infarction, bradycardias will occur if there is impairment of the sinus node branch of the right or left coronary artery (sinus bradycardia), or of the AV nodal branch of the right

56

coronary artery (some degree of heart block) (Figure 13). In addition, the pain of the infarction or its accompanying pericarditis may stimulate the vagus nerve to cause a bradycardia.

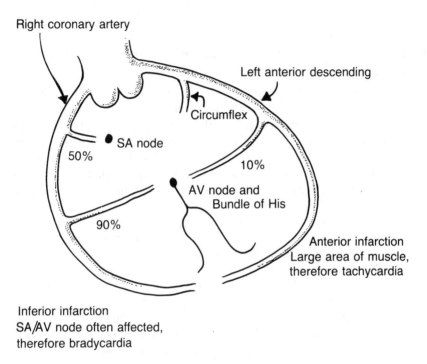

Figure 13   *Heart rate and site of infarction.*

A right coronary artery occlusion will result in an inferior infarction, and this is more likely to be associated with a bradycardia than an anterior infarction (left coronary artery). An anterior infarction tends to be associated with a tachycardia, because there is usually a relatively large area of myocardial damage.

Fats

76. At what level of cholesterol or lipid profile would you actively advise dietary change? Cholesterol-lowering medication?

A few years ago the answer would have been simple – a cholesterol greater than 7.5mmol/l or triglycerides greater than 4mmol/l. This recommendation still stands for the 'non-believer' of the diet-heart theory, for all patients under the age of sixty-five. However, the evidence of a number of trials of cholesterol, triglycerides, diet and drug therapy in the prevention of ischaemic heart disease suggests that we should be stricter with our criteria, for example: cholesterol > 6.5mmol/l, triglycerides > 2.5mmol/l.

If your laboratory sends out a lipid profile result you can be more accurate in deciding who *must* stick to a diet. Total cholesterol can be divided into very low density lipoproteins (VLDL), low density lipoproteins (LDL) and high density lipoproteins (HDL). LDL cholesterol levels correlate very positively with ischaemic heart disease, and LDL is therefore the principal 'baddy'. HDL is protective against cardiovascular disease, and the higher the level the better. It is, therefore, the 'goody'. In terms of ratio, if the HDL is 20% or more of the LDL level, the cardiovascular risk diminishes. The LDL can be calculated according to the formula:

$$LDL = \text{Total Cholesterol} - \left(HDL + \frac{\text{Triglycerides}}{2 \cdot 19}\right) \text{mmol/l}$$

Is it worth bothering with this formula? If the LDL is greater than 5, the patient has type II hyperlipoproteinaemia or familial hypercholesterolaemia (the family history often talked about on TV). These patients most certainly need a diet, and if this fails to lower the cholesterol, cholestyramine would be the drug of choice, although it is often unpleasant to take. If the LDL is less than 5mmol/l, but the triglycerides are greater than 2.5mmol/l, this is type IV hyperlipoproteinaemia. If diet fails, the standard practice is treatment with bezafibrate. Isolated raised triglycerides should be treated by diet alone.

77. **A patient has a sudden unannounced coronary death. You have no figures on the deceased's lipid status before death. Is there any age at death below which you would consider it justified to examine the blood of his children for hyperlipidaemia?**

It is advisable to examine the blood for hyperlipidaemia in the children of a parent whose first cardiovascular event (which may be death, as in this question) occurs before the age of sixty-five years. It is also advisable to do so if an uncle or aunt dies before fifty-five years of age. Factors which would make you more likely to find a positive result are if the child is obese, smokes, or has a parent or brother or sister who has diabetes.

78. **Two men of thirty-eight. Both are fit with reasonable family histories. They both apply for life insurance. One has had a recent health check revealing a cholesterol of 9.4. How much more loading is the insurance company likely to apply to his proposal, compared to that of the man whose cholesterol status is unknown?**

If an insurance company is aware that a man of thirty-eight has a fasting cholesterol of 9.4, they would load him between 70–90%. If they do not have this information, and in all other respects the man is healthy and a non-smoker, he will not be loaded. In this situation it seems sensible not to check someone's cholesterol until after the insurance premium has been agreed!

79. **Is there any age above which you would not advise a patient with a relatively normal lipid profile to change his dietary habits? Is there any advantage in a man of forty changing over from a diet in which he eats moderate amounts of dairy products to one in which he eats more polyunsaturates?**

After the age of sixty-five it is almost certainly not worth bothering about blood lipids at all. There is certainly no advantage in reducing them. Under the age of sixty-five the story is very different. The upper limits of normal for blood cholesterol are proportional to age:

30 years	6.5mmol/l
30–50 years	7.0mmol/l
50–65 years	7.5mmol/l

The upper limit of triglycerides is 2.5mmol/l. It is important that the triglycerides measurement is fasting (14 hours of water only), or the results may be grossly inaccurate. If your laboratory can do fractionation of cholesterols, the upper limit of normal is an LDL cholesterol of 5mmol/l, especially if the HDL/LDL ratio is less that 0.2. HDL cholesterol is protective, whereas both LDL and VLDL are not. The greater the ratio of HDL to LDL and VLDL the better.

Diet is the mainstay of treatment. The aim is to obtain less than 30% of the daily calorific intake from fat and to increase the proportion of polyunsaturates. Only if the cholesterol remains outside the normal range after three months on a proper diet should drugs be considered. At present, either bezafibrate or cholestyramine is the favoured medication.

If the cholesterol is normal, altering the diet is of limited value, although it is true to say that the lower the cholesterol the lower the risk of ischaemic heart disease. There are two possible approaches to the population at large. Either one can seek out those most at risk and treat them individually, or one can advise everyone to adopt a more prudent diet. For large populations the former is very expensive, and the latter more efficient overall. In general practice it may be possible to identify those at risk, looking particularly for those with a bad family history.

Sudden Death

80. Is sudden, completely unannounced cardiac death as common as it would seem, or is it generally considered that there is some kind of warning in the form of pre-coronary syndrome? If there is such a syndrome, what action should be taken when its presence is suspected?

Officially there is no pre-coronary syndrome, or we would all be very conscious of it. Most patients who have a coronary, even those with alleged sudden death, have probably had some prior chest pain which they have dismissed as indigestion, and almost all patients have undue fatigue for several months before the event. Unfortunately, neither of these are specific enough to be of value. All one can say is that in a patient who is at high risk, and who simply doesn't feel quite well, one should maintain a high level of watchfulness.

81. You are called to see a man of forty-five who has collapsed. When you arrive there is no pulse or respiration, nor is there an expert observer to say how long this has been so. Are there any contraindications to attempting resuscitation? If not, how long would you continue without success? How long after a cardiac arrest might respiration continue?

In a man of forty-five you must begin resuscitation unless there is an observer to tell you that he has terminal cancer or something similar. You cannot assume that the brain may be irreparably damaged because more than the statutory three minutes have elapsed. There are many cases of excellent recovery after apparent death for ten minutes or more.

It is said that cardiac massage produces only a relatively small flow of blood to the brain, and that this in theory is inadequate – and yet patients are regularly and completely resuscitated in this way. In a young man it is important to continue cardiopulmonary resuscitation for perhaps up to an hour. In practice you should continue until you can get the patient transported to hospital, where a formal assessment of his ECG can be made. I have personally restarted a patient to a normal life after an hour and ten minutes resuscitation. Medicine is full of such surprises.

If you do decide to abandon resuscitation, agonal breathing usually

61

ceases abruptly and certainly within a few minutes. Occasionally that awful situation occurs where a patient suddenly starts to breathe again after the resuscitation team has just walked away. This is nerve-racking, as everybody has to start all over again. Usually it is to no avail and fortunately is very rare.

One change in the practice of resuscitation which has occurred in the last few years concerns the relative number of compressions of the chest (cardiac massage), compared with the number of inflations of the chest. Traditionally this has been five compressions of the chest to every inflation of the chest. Research shows that only after two or three compressions is there any flow of blood at all to the brain.

Once cardiac massage is started, it is continuous. If you are alone you should carry out two inflations and then fifteen compressions. This should be repeated until a decision to stop is made. If help is available, the ratio of compressions to inflations is 5:1, but there must be no interruption to the rhythm of compression. Full details are available in *The ABC of Resuscitation*, published by the British Medical Journal with contributions from the Resuscitation Council (UK).

82. How long after a respiratory arrest might cardiac function continue?

I doubt if anyone knows the answer to this. In the sleep apnoea syndrome, where patients may stop breathing for 1–2 minutes, arrhythmias have been shown to occur, but the heart does not stop. It is probable that the heart would stop after 3–5 minutes, but pure respiratory arrest is very rare indeed. It is likely to be limited to patients with chronic obstructive airways disease whose blood gases become severely disturbed.

83. Tricyclic antidepressants have a certain reputation for being associated with sudden cardiac death. As many patients with ischaemic heart disease have some degree of depression, should this not be a consideration when their treatment is being decided upon?

Tricyclic antidepressants cause an increase in catecholamines centrally, which in part is presumably how they work. In addition they are cholinergic and antihistaminic. Thus a variety of symptoms and side effects are likely, such as dry mouth, disturbances of vision and micturition, tachycardia and tremor. In ischaemic heart disease there is need for special care with this drug, because it can give rise to a variety of arrhythmias, usually tachycardias, possibly resulting in angina and even sudden death. Such episodes are extremely uncommon and it is reasonable to say that tricyclic antidepressants are only contraindicated in the severest cases. Tricyclics must be avoided if you think a patient with ischaemic heart disease may take an overdose because the depression is severe, as serious arrhythmias are relatively frequent in any tricyclic overdosage.

84. **A previously fit man of fifty-two suddenly clutches his chest, complains of intense pain and within a minute is dead. Is the doctor justified in certifying cause of death as an acute myocardial infarction without any further evidence? If the man had seen a doctor for a completely unassociated matter twelve days before, should the doctor sign a cremation certificate without notifying the coroner's officer?**

Severe chest pain followed by sudden death is of course most likely to be due to a sudden myocardial infarction. However, it could be a pulmonary embolus, dissecting aneurysm of the ascending aorta, myocarditis with pericarditis, rupture of the mitral valve and so on. In addition, poisoning of some description is always a possibility, and one is reluctant to be didactic about the cause of sudden death in this case. An intracranial bleed may result in abrupt death, though not usually with chest pain, and one can dream up a variety of curious possibilities. In these situations it is undoubtedly wise to inform the coroner's officer before signing any death certificate.

85. **What is the mechanism of sudden cardiac death in circumstances such as jogging? Is there any way in which this disaster might be foreseen and avoided? What other circumstances are associated with sudden coronary death?**

It seems fair say that most deaths due to jogging fall into two groups – the younger patient from teenager upwards, and the older patient, the 'has been' or MMSS (male menopausal syndrome sufferer).

Deaths in the younger age group are likely to be due to a myocarditis. Occasionally a prolonged Q-T syndrome or Wolff-Parkinson-White syndrome may result in sudden death, but these serious conditions tend to present very early on in life with tachycardias or blackouts. Myocarditis is more common than is generally supposed, even though very few people will actually come to any harm. Every year, unfortunately, there are at least a few unnecessary deaths in young men who develop ventricular fibrillation whilst running during a virus infection. It is thought that the virus interferes with energy production within the myocardial cell, so that metabolic acidosis occurs easily and arrhythmias rapidly develop.

The important advice to give to all joggers, irrespective of age, is not to run when they have a cold or similar viral infection. Few people ever seem to take this advice, preferring to 'run off' their fever.

In the older age group, ventricular fibrillation during exercise is more likely to occur from ischaemic heart disease (the 'gym didn't fix it' syndrome).

How can such a disaster be prevented? It is certainly not possible to stop all such deaths, but it is vital to encourage joggers to report any abnormal symptoms, particularly chest pain or undue dyspnoea and fatigue. A resting ECG is so often normal, whatever the state of the heart, that it is virtually useless. An exercise ECG can be very misleading in an asymptomatic patient, and most authorities feel that exercise testing before allowing someone to go jogging is unnecessary. A careful history, making sure that there is no suggestion of ischaemic heart disease, followed by a very gradual introduction to the exercise itself, is the only safe approach. It might be worth looking more carefully into those at greater risk, such as smokers with a family history of ischaemic heart disease, but in most districts there is in any case very little access to exercise testing.

Occasionally more complicated heart conditions are associated with sudden death, e.g. hypertrophic obstructive cardiomyopathy, aortic stenosis, or dilated cardiomyopathy. There is probably no way of avoiding these tragedies.

Other conditions associated with sudden death are occasions of extreme emotion, for example when threatened with being mugged, having to make a speech at an important function, flying in an aeroplane if one is an agoraphobic, or making love to one's mistress. It is doubtful if all these could be avoided, so that other than telling a patient to use his common sense there is little one can do.

Leaky Valves

86. Is there any form of immunisation a patient with congenital or rheumatic heart defect should *not* receive at any age? What about after a myocardial infarction?

Except in patients who are severely ill with congenital, rheumatic or ischaemic heart disease, there is no contraindication to immunisation. The occasional toxic reaction to immunisation may tip the balance in a patient who has, for example, severe heart failure, but the great majority of patients will tolerate the procedure perfectly well.

In practical terms it is only on the very rare occasion that children, for a cardiological reason, are unable to have their normal protective immunisation – tetanus, diphtheria, whooping cough, polio and measles.

87. What type of patient with valvular heart disease with *no* previous history of embolic phenomena would you treat with long-term anticoagulants?

Rheumatic mitral valve disease, whether stenosis or incompetence, carries a 30% risk of systemic embolus over a lifetime. It is often assumed that this is only likely to be the case if the patient is in atrial fibrillation, but the risk is no less in sinus rhythm. As a general rule one begins to anticoagulate patients with rheumatic mitral valve disease after the age of forty, when atrial fibrillation is in any case likely to develop. In women one has to assume that childbearing has finished by this age, since warfarin cannot be used during pregnancy.

You will note that I refer only to 'rheumatic' mitral valve disease. This is the only likely pathology, since the other form – congenital mitral stenosis – is extremely rare and would almost certainly have presented in childhood. If a patient has mitral stenosis and is over forty, anticoagulate without further ado.

There are many causes of mitral incompetence. Perhaps the commonest is functional, when a failing left ventricle dilates the mitral ring. This disappears as the failure is treated. The billowing mitral leaflet syndrome is also a common cause (see Question 90). Mitral incom-

65

petence occurs congenitally, both alone and with other congenital lesions, for example ASD. It is associated with such conditions as Marfan's syndrome and may occur with both infective endocarditis and rheumatic fever. Nevertheless, the large majority which are not functional are rheumatic in origin.

If you find mitral valve disease, should you anticoagulate the patient yourself, or refer on to a cardiologist? I personally think it is important for the patient to be assessed fully at the earliest possible stage with an ECG, CXR and echocardiograph (an ultrasound recording of the heart showing valve movements and the chamber sizes). In this case it is also reasonable for the hospital to begin anticoagulation, although how it is followed up depends on local circumstances.

There has long been much argument as to which patients with atrial fibrillation should be anticoagulated. The current feeling is that those with mitral valve disease, thyrotoxicosis or a previous systemic embolus must be treated, but that is about all. Lone atrial fibrillation (no cause found) does have an incidence of systemic emboli, but since 10% of the elderly population have atrial fibrillation it would be practically impossible to start anticoagulating great numbers of patients as well as cope with all the haemorrhagic consequences.

88. An asymptomatic woman of thirty-five is found on examination to have mitral stenosis. At what stage in the development of her disease would you advise surgery?

The decision to operate on mitral stenosis (as well as on mitral incompetence and aortic incompetence, but *not* aortic stenosis – see Question 92) depends almost entirely on symptoms. As the stenosis gets tighter, dyspnoea and fatigue will worsen. If a patient finds that he or she cannot walk up a flight of stairs without stopping for breath, then you have probably left it too late. If the patient has to stop at the top of the stairs you must certainly get on with it. Paroxysmal nocturnal dyspnoea and orthopnoea also indicate that it is time to consider an operation. However, we are not considering a patient who is entirely untreated. We are assuming that these symptoms are present in spite of, say, 80mg of frusemide or the equivalent being taken. If you need to use more diuretic than this then you should consider operation.

It is not uncommon for patients with mitral valve disease to get suddenly worse. This does not necessarily indicate a tightening of the valve. It is more likely that the patient has gone into sudden atrial fibrillation.

What about examination? Can you assess the severity of mitral stenosis by auscultation? This is perfectly possible but does need a fair amount of experience. The crucial factor is the gap between the second heart sound (P_2) and the opening snap (OS). The shorter this gap, the tighter the stenosis. In a practical sense, if you can hear a gap it is almost certainly mild mitral stenosis; if you cannot detect a gap it is probably tight mitral stenosis (Figure 14).

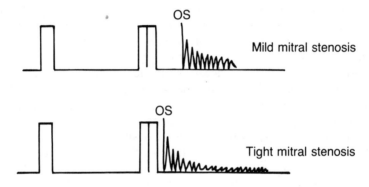

Figure 14   *The severity of mitral stenosis.*

A loud P_2 represents pulmonary hypertension and therefore at least significant mitral stenosis. This would be accompanied by a right ventricular heave. The loudness of the murmur is irrelevant. It is a question of 'length before strength'. Note that the presystolic murmur is also irrelevant. This only represents pliability, and contrary to almost all textbooks *is* present in atrial fibrillation as well as in sinus rhythm. The value of this sign is that it means you may be able to split the valve rather than do a valve replacement.

In a women of thirty-five it would be unlikely that the mitral stenosis was tight. In Caucasians, symptoms rarely develop before the mid-forties. In Africans it may be considerably earlier. If the symptoms are significant in a woman of thirty-five it may be because she is pregnant, but it is still possible to do a valvotomy or valve replacement if necessary.

89. It is well known that people with congenital and rheumatic heart disease should have antibiotic cover during dental treatment. What other situations, surgical or medical, should be similarly covered?

There are still a significant number of cases of infective endocarditis every year in the UK, and the mortality rate remains depressingly high (up to 50%). It is vital, therefore, to adhere to the practice of antibiotic cover for surgical and dental procedures.

In dental practice it is probably only necessary to give such cover for tooth extraction, root filling and vigorous scaling. However, if in doubt, give antibiotics. It is true that even chewing gum can result in a bacteraemia. If you give the antibiotic too early you will remove the sensitive bacteria and allow possible infection with more resistant bacteria. Therefore antibiotics *must* be given 30-60 minutes before the procedure starts. It is not necessary in dental practice to give intramuscular antibiotics. Current practice is 3g amoxycillin orally ½–1 hour before the procedure and 3g amoxycillin eight hours later. If the patient is allergic to penicillin, use erythromycin 1g orally instead.

Antibiotics cover must be given for *any* surgical procedure, and this includes the delivery of a baby. Because there is likely to be a wide variety of possible infecting organisms, including gram negative bacteria, gentamicin 80mg should be given intramuscular ½–1 hour before the surgical procedure and then 8-hourly for 48 hours. During childbirth the first dose should be given just before the second stage.

90. What is the mitral leaflet syndrome? When should it be suspected?

The mitral leaflet syndrome was first fully described by Professor J. Barlow of Johannesburg in the 1960s, hence one of its names 'Barlow's syndrome'. It is also known as the 'billowing mitral leaflet syndrome', 'the parachute leaflet syndrome' and 'ruptured cusp of the mitral valve'. There are three degrees of the syndrome. In its mildest form one cusp balloons out in systolic, and as it snaps open it gives a midsystolic click (Figure 15).

If the chordae tendineae are elongated the click will occur, but the cusps will not remain in opposition in late systole, and mitral incompetence will result (Figure 16). This gives a late systolic murmur. In this situation the murmur is often very loud but the incompetence is not severe.

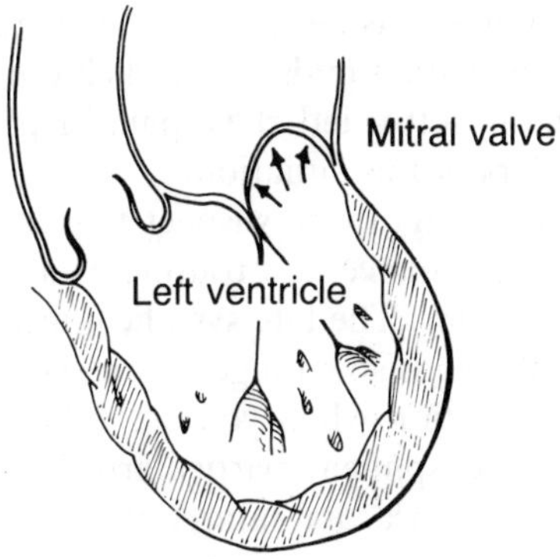

Figure 15
The billowing mitral leaflet syndrome with no mitral incompetence.

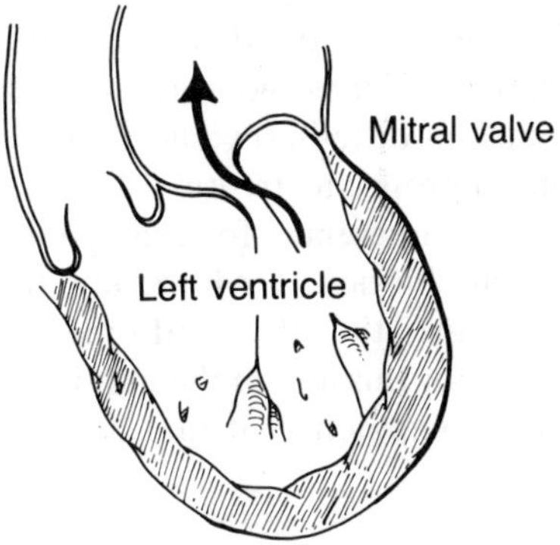

Figure 16
The billowing mitral leaflet syndrome with mild mitral incompetence.

If the chordae have ruptured there will be a pansystolic murmur of considerable mitral incompetence (Figure 17). Such rupture may occur with a myocardial infarction, rheumatic fever, infective endocarditis and collagen disorders. Rupture is usually preceded by an elongation of the chordae. Sudden complete rupture has a high mortality unless repaired surgically in the first eight hours.

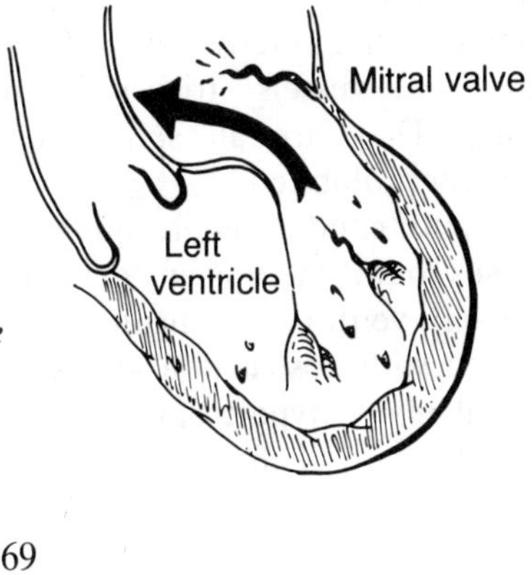

Figure 17
The billowing mitral leaflet syndrome with moderate to severe mitral incompetence.

Symptoms thus depend on the degree of mitral incompetence. However, patients with a midsystolic click only, for reasons which are obscure, are prone to left-sided chest pain or palpitations. Beta-blockers often work wonders in this situation.

When might one suspect that a patient has this condition? Most are found by chance at a routine examination, either by hearing the click or the murmur. The late systolic murmur often sounds like a cooing dove or seagull and is so strange that it should alert one instantly. You might find this condition when you are called to see a patient who has developed sudden dyspnoea, particularly if associated with chest pain. After an inferior myocardial infarction, rupture of the posterior cusp of the mitral valve is quite frequently reported. It is worth listening for these distinctive heart sounds in any patient who is complaining of dyspnoea and fatigue. For no good reason many patients with this condition seem to complain of lethargy and tiredness.

The appropriate treatment is the same as that for any patient with mitral incompetence, for example diuretics for dyspnoea. It is important to give antibiotic cover for dental treatment or surgery. There have been some reports that the syndrome may cause sudden death. There is no evidence for this and in the majority of cases, depending on the degree of mitral incompetence, it runs a very benign course.

91. Should any restriction be placed on a child with a minor congenital cardiac defect that causes no symptoms on rest or exercise?

No. If the congenital defect really is minor then there should be no danger at all. But how do you know? Congenital heart disease can be divided into blue and pink.

All the conditions in the blue group are notable for cyanosis and for beginning with T – tetralogy of Fallot, truncus arteriosus, transposition of the great vessels, tricuspid atresia and total anomalous venous drainage. They are all serious conditions and vigorous exercise is completely prohibited.

Most pink conditions are quite safe, e.g. ASD, VSD, patent ductus arteriosus, but if there is any evidence of obstruction to the outflow tract of the left ventricle, difficulties may occur on exercise. The lesions associated with obstruction are aortic stenosis – valvular, supravalvular or subvalvular – hypertrophic obstructive cardiomyopathy (HOCM) or tight coarctation of the aorta (Figure 18).

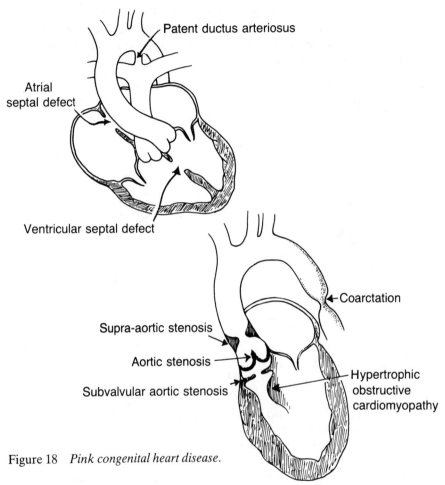

Patent ductus arteriosus

Atrial septal defect

Ventricular septal defect

Coarctation

Supra-aortic stenosis

Aortic stenosis

Subvalvular aortic stenosis

Hypertrophic obstructive cardiomyopathy

Figure 18   *Pink congenital heart disease.*

HOCM is an excessive enlargement of ventricular muscle of poor quality which closes down on itself, preventing blood escaping from the ventricle. When exercise is taken the peripheral arterioles vasodilate and reduce the afterload. This, in turn, increases the gradient across the obstruction and raises the left ventricular end diastolic pressure. This can lead to severe heart failure. It is only likely to occur if the obstruction is at least moderate, and is difficult to assess without sophisticated equipment and possible cardiac catheterisation. To be on the safe side, exercise should be prohibited in these conditions until a formal assessment and diagnosis has been made.

92. A man of sixty-six with minimal symptoms of heart failure, i.e. slightly increased breathlessness on exercise, is found to have a calcified aortic valve. What considerations should be made on whether or not he should have aortic valve replacement?

Aortic stenosis is the one valve lesion that you have to be extremely diligent about. The natural history of aortic stenosis is that symptoms do not develop until a late stage, when there is often rapid deterioration and sudden death (Figure 19).

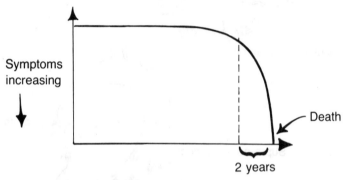

Figure 19   *The natural history of aortic stenosis.*

The symptoms of aortic stenosis are the four A's: angina, asthma (cardiac), attacks of unconsciousness and arrhythmias. The onset of any of these symptoms suggests death may occur within two years. If a patient with aortic stenosis is getting breathless it suggests left ventricular failure. This is very serious. Death may occur very quickly indeed, and if there is overt pulmonary oedema it is often necessary to do an emergency aortic valve replacement.

The development of left ventricular hypertrophy and strain on the ECG also suggests impending problems, even without symptoms. Beware aortic stenosis! Any patient with aortic stenosis must be followed up carefully and referred to the local cardiac clinic if symptoms occur.

The X-ray appearance of a calcified aortic valve does *not* necessarily represent aortic stenosis. Again, the length before strength rule applies. The *long* murmur is likely to be aortic stenosis, the short murmur, aortic sclerosis – a totally benign condition.

Miscellaneous

93. Does vigorous exercise too soon after an acute virus infection such as influenza make myocarditis any more likely? Are there any infections in which the possible consequence of myocarditis should be particularly looked out for?

There is no evidence for this. As a general rule it is unwise to exercise during the acute stages of a viral infection. Not because it might induce myocarditis, but because myocarditis might already be present. The only virus commonly associated with myocarditis is Coxsackie B, which presents non-specifically, and so it is only when pericarditis and myocarditis develop that the possibility of such an infection is suspected.

94. Is there an association between low body temperature, e.g. a minor degree of hypothermia in an elderly person, and an increased prevalence of ischaemic heart disease?

So far as is known, the genesis of atheroma is not in any way related to cold weather or hypothermia. However, the cold may help to worsen ischaemic heart disease or precipitate an infarction. A cold external temperature vasoconstricts the skin vessels. This in turn causes a reflex vasoconstriction of the coronary vessels. Hence angina is always worse in the cold weather, and in extreme circumstances an infarction may occur.

Once hypothermia (body temperature below 35°C) has developed, the oxygenation of tissues becomes impaired and arrhythmias are likely. There is also an accumulation of lactic acid caused by shivering, giving rise to a metabolic acidosis as well as an increase in potassium. Between 28°C and 35°C atrial fibrillation is not uncommon. However, below 28°C ventricular fibrillation is more likely.

95. A patient returns to the doctor and says that he has been told at the hospital that he has 'Syndrome X'. What is it? How is the condition to be explained to him?

Syndrome X is typical clinical angina pectoris occurring in a patient with normal coronary arteries and with no evidence of coronary artery spasm.

It usually comes to light when a patient who has chest pain and a positive exercise test is referred for coronary angiography, and is found to have surprisingly normal or near-normal coronary arteries. Later in the procedure an intravenous injection of ergonovine may be given. In the normal subject there will be about a 30% vasoconstriction of the coronary arteries. In a patient whose underlying problem is coronary artery spasm, the vessels will constrict vigorously, often with pain, or even disappear altogether. Rapid infusion of IV nitrate reduces the spasm quickly and only very rarely is there any residual problem. In Syndrome X there is only the normal degree of spasm.

There is no adequate explanation for this condition in the absence of blocked arteries and abnormal spasm, even though radioisotope studies confirm that there *is* ischaemia. It is presumed that the defect is cellular and that, in some way, energy production is faulty. It is tempting to think that the problem, like everything else nowadays, can be blamed on the poor old virus.

Treating Syndrome X is very difficult. There is no particular drug of choice and one often has to ring the changes of all antianginal therapy from time to time. Relief is only moderate and the symptoms can vary a great deal from month to month. One important fact with which one can reassure patients is that they are no more likely to drop dead than anybody else and can expect to live a normal lifespan.

96. The pain is atypical, the ECG is unhelpful, beds are short. Is there a place for doing cardiac enzymes in a GP setting? How valuable a guide are they? How do they vary over the period of illness or non-illness?

The most valuable diagnostic enzyme from the cardiac point of view is the MB fraction of creatinine phosphokinase (MB-CPK). Its rise in the blood stream is almost totally limited to that caused by myocardial damage. Previously, creatinine phosphokinase (CPK) and lactic dehydrogenase (LDH) were used, but a rise in these enzymes can be caused by other pathologies. Any muscle damage, including an intramuscular injection, will raise the CPK, and LDH is raised by pulmonary emboli, damage to red cells (haemolysis) and other conditions. Biochemistry departments often estimate all three enzymes as well as the aspartate serum transaminase (AST), so that an overall view of possible cardiac damage can be assessed. Each enzyme appears in the blood stream at a slightly different rate (Figure 20).

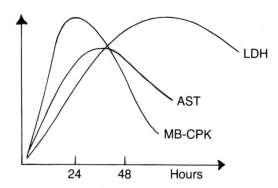

Figure 20   *The release of serum enzymes after a myocardial infarction.*

Because MB-CPK is the most accurate of the enzymes in relation to heart disease, as well as being the first to appear in the blood stream, it is the enzyme of choice in the diagnosis of chest pains. In general practice there are bound to be a number of occasions when a patient with chest pain is not admitted to hospital. In these cases a diagnosis can only be made by ECG or an enzyme estimation. The ECG may be normal or equivocal, or else be difficult to interpret with confidence.

An enzyme estimation taken at the time of the pain, followed by another twenty-four hours later, can be extremely valuable. Ideally a rise and fall is looked for. This will require three estimations, although an MB-CPK above the normal limit is usually significant even on its own. A later rise of the other enzymes confirms the suspicion of an infarction. Samples taken in the evening and left overnight before analysis tend to be less accurate, because of haemolysis due to shaking, but are still helpful (the more so with careful handling).

97. It is usually assumed by the doctor that crepitations at one base signify pneumonia, and that at both bases they signify left ventricular failure. Can left ventricular failure be represented by unilateral basal crepitations? If so is it more likely on one side than the other?

Crepitations are usually divided into fine (pulmonary oedema) and coarse (infection). Fine crepitations appear to be caused by the opening of collapsed alveoli. Their collapse, in turn, is due to interstitial oedema. As the patient takes a deep breath, the alveoli burst open and crackle. The interstitial oedema is present at the bases of the lungs because of gravity. If the patient with failure was, like Father William, to stand on his head, the crepitations would be at the apices. In much the same way, if the chest is examined after the patient has been lying on his side for any length of time, the crepitations will be, predominantly, on that side.

Do not forget that the basal alveoli will tend to collapse in almost anyone who is slumped in a chair for quite a while. Crepitations will be audible if you listen to the bases without asking the patient to cough first. After a couple of good coughs, crepitations due simply to stasis will clear.

Coarse crepitations will always remain at the site of infection, and instead of being a fine regular crackling will be loud and intermittent. Fever is not an indication that crepitations are purely infective in origin, because as a general rule pulmonary oedema will become infected after twenty-four hours. To be perfectly honest, a chest X-ray is infinitely preferable to any pair of ears in these circumstances.

98. What proportion of cases of pericarditis have an underlying myocardial infarction? If there is no evidence of infarction is the patient able to take exercise as soon as the pain has gone?

The commonest cause of pericarditis in the middle-aged and older patient is a myocardial infarction. In the younger patient it is probably benign viral pericarditis.

Because dead myocardium is surrounded by an inflammatory reaction, it is reasonably common for a pericarditis to occur as part of a myocardial infarction. This is often found accidently by hearing a pericardial friction rub. True pericardial pain is the exception rather than the rule. It is said that as many as 15% of infarctions are followed by at least a short period of pericarditis.

The presence of pericarditis after a myocardial infarction has no special prognostic significance. The same rules apply to mobilisation as would apply after any other infarction. When listening to the praecordium in this situation, it is not easy to differentiate between a murmur (e.g. mitral incompetence) and a friction rub. As a general rule, the friction rub will remain equally audible however hard you press the diaphragm of your stethoscope on the skin. A murmur of any description will get fainter the harder you press.

Benign viral pericarditis is a pain in every sense of the word. It usually occurs in young people, presenting with a typical pericardial pain – i.e. it is central, worse on deep breathing or coughing and is often made better by a change of position, either lying down or sitting up. The pain usually lasts up to seven to ten days, is uncomfortable rather than severe, responds well to non-steroidal anti-inflammatory drugs, and if it is absolutely necessary to use them, to steroids.

The problems with viral pericarditis are twofold. Firstly the pain may be recurrent, particularly in the early weeks, and the patient often gets rather depressed. Secondly, there is frequently an underlying myocarditis which manifests itself as fatigue and lethargy rather than as any failure. As a general rule these patients must wait for the fatigue and lethargy to disappear, rather than the pain, before they exercise. Vigorous exercise with myocarditis is dangerous, particularly if pain is present.

The typical changes of the ECG in pericarditis are the raised ST segments with upright T waves (Figure 21):

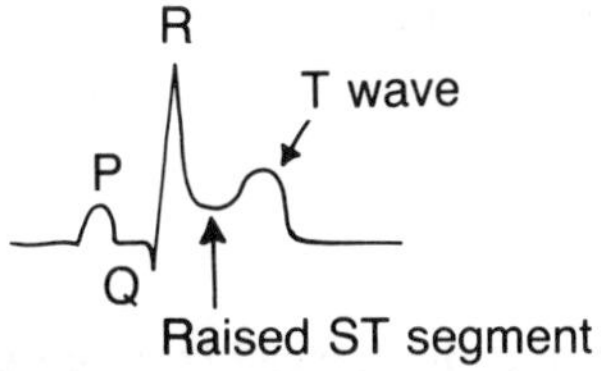

Figure 21   *The ECG of pericarditis.*

Whilst this is the appearance of pericarditis it is also present in the early stages of myocardial infarction. However, it is also seen in patients with an athletic heart and is a normal variation in West Indians and Africans.

99. You have been shipwrecked on a desert island with a group of fellow passengers, in varying degrees of health. You are allowed three cardiologically active drugs. Which would you choose, and why?

My three drugs of choice would be:

1) Digoxin.
2) A diuretic (frusemide or bumetanide).
3) A beta-blocker/calcium antagonist combination,
   e.g. atenolol/nifedipine.

The choice of drug depends upon the situation you are most likely to encounter. These are: cardiac failure, arrhythmia, angina pectoris and hypertension.

Digoxin can be most useful in the treatment of cardiac failure, particularly if the cause of that failure is atrial fibrillation. Although its use in heart failure associated with sinus rhythm remains controversial, in practice it does seem effective. Since the commonest arrhythmia is AF it is clearly of value, as well as being useful in many supraventricular tachyarrhythmias. In resistant arrhythmias, many of which are ischaemic in origin, digoxin can be used to good effect with beta-blocker/calcium antagonist combinations.

Angina pectoris and hypertension should be controlled by the beta-blocker/calcium antagonist combination. In resistant hypertension, however, the diuretic might also be required. Acute heart failure is the most serious cardiovascular emergency likely to be encountered, so a powerful diuretic is essential. Small doses would keep chronic heart failure under control.

100. An elderly gentleman is discharged from hospital to his bed-sitter. He has been fitted with a pacemaker. Prior to admission he had acquired a microwave oven. He asks whether his pacemaker could be affected by the microwaves. What happens if it breaks down? How long do the batteries last?

Microwaves are high-intensity electromagnetic radio waves which can switch off a pacemaker if close contact occurs. In practice, this is only likely if the microwave oven is 'leaky'. It is nevertheless advisable to tell a patient with a pacemaker not to use one.

Most pacemakers inserted nowadays have lithium-iodine cells with a titanium surround and weigh about 40g. The battery lasts between seven and ten years. The average life expectancy of the elderly patient who requires a pacemaker is seven years, so there is little point in developing a battery which lasts much longer. After one month the pacemaker must be checked and its electrical parameters noted, using a special instrument. Any changes in these parameters will be found at the annual check-up, and if the batteries appear to be running down the pacemaker can be changed.

One of the possible consequences of pacemaker failure is sudden death. Another is the equivalent of a Stokes-Adams attack. The patient, without warning, falls to the ground in asystole, but after two minutes or so the idiopathic ventricular pacemaker will take over at about 30-40 beats per minute and the patient will gradually regain consciousness. He will in effect be back in complete heart block and is, of course, still susceptible to repeated Stokes-Adams attacks. As a matter of urgency a temporary pacemaker must be inserted, so immediate referral to hospital is vital.

Index

Please note: the numbers in this index refer to question numbers, and not to pagination.

Index

— NOTES —

— NOTES —

— NOTES —

— NOTES —

7, 19, 27, 70, 71, 76, 79, 100.